ONE WEEK LOAN

D1513638

10

interior details for the home
and where to find them

Ian Rudge and Geraldine Rudge

1000
interior details for the home
and where to find them

Laurence King Publishing

LAURENCE KING

© text 2009 Ian Rudge and Geraldine Rudge
Published in 2009 by Laurence King Publishing Ltd

361–373 City Road
London EC1V 1LR
United Kingdom
Tel: + 44 20 7841 6900
Fax: + 44 20 7841 6910
email: enquiries@laurenceking.com
www.laurenceking.com

A catalogue record for this book is
available from the British Library.

ISBN-13: 978 1 85669 610 4

Picture research by Angelina Li
Design by Rudd Studio

Printed in China

Front Cover: DNA chandelier by Benjamin Hopf and
Constantin Wortmann of Buro Fur Form for Next.

For Evan and Theo

Note: all imperial measurements are
rounded to the nearest half-unit.

→
Contents

INTRODUCTION

With the help of more than 1000 illuminating images, this book looks at every aspect of interior detail for the home. Whether you are an interior designer, an architect or simply a lover of modern design, it offers a wealth of information, including many of the best and most innovative products launched all over the world since the beginning of the twenty-first century. The aim is to showcase the latest cutting-edge developments and to provide ideas and inspiration for every domestic space.

This is not, however, purely a glossy picture book. Each chapter is introduced by an interview with a leading designer whose advice, opinions and comments are essential reading for anyone planning to make changes to a domestic space. All the contributors have been highly influential in shaping the look of the contemporary home.

The continuing revolution in how we use our kitchens is one of the first subjects to be put in the spotlight. Increasingly, the open-plan kitchen is an integral part of a living space, reflecting changing attitudes to food preparation and eating. We want kitchens that enhance but don't dominate, that are subtle in design, and that in some cases are reduced to a single free-standing item – a piece of furniture rather than a suite of kitchen cabinets.

Dramatic changes have also taken place in the bathroom – no longer a cold, tiled, utilitarian environment where damp is the only thing that lingers. Indeed, the modern bathroom may emulate a luxurious spa, where nature is replicated by a shower that mimics rain or a waterfall, where water is illuminated by LED effects to sooth or stimulate our senses, and where aromatherapy and hydrotherapy are available at the flick of a switch. There is a bath that doubles as a loudspeaker and a self-closing lavatory that plays music as well as washing, drying and deodorizing the user on demand.

Robin Levien, whose interview introduces chapter on bathrooms (chapter five), is an expert in industrial ceramics who, through his work for Ideal Standard, designs one quarter of all the bathroom suites sold in the UK. Levien is preoccupied by 'future-proofing' – the elusive task of trying to determine what we will demand of home products in the future and what the needs of an ageing population will be. Contemporary designers are increasingly taking account of the entire life cycle of a product, the 'womb-to-tomb' or 'cradle-to-grave' concept, as it is known. This results in products, many illustrated in this book, that are durable, flexible and enduring – and easier to recycle.

For Levien, future-proofing does not mean compromising on aesthetics. When we spoke to him, he was designing a prototype bath that was elegant enough to enhance any contemporary bathroom. Yet that same design, with simple modifications, would also accommodate the needs of young children or people with disabilities. For Levien, who initially trained as a ceramist, there is little difference between designing a bath and executing a piece of sculpture.

An interest in materials and in the act of making is a recurrent theme. The German kitchen designer Norbert Wangen, whose designs are produced by Boffi, also emphasizes the importance of understanding the processes involved in making new products. Wangen was in the vanguard of those designers who broke free from the constraints of traditional kitchen concepts in the 1990s, responding to popular demand for a less formal demarcation line between eating and living areas. His seminal monoblock kitchen, K4, was a solitary piece of sculptural furniture whose functional aspects were concealed inside. It was no surprise to learn that Wangen, who also designs furniture, had studied sculpture.

Bathroom and kitchen fixtures are made in an ever-wider range of materials, including manmade composites such as Corian, Durat, Cristalplant and LG Hi-Macs that can be moulded into seamless sculptural forms in an infinite range of shapes and colours. High-tech laminates and coatings such as those used in the Z-Island Kitchen by Zaha Hadid are also transforming the domestic landscape. Hadid's futuristic kitchen is a 'sensory-responsive kitchen environment', with high-tech coatings providing sound, light and heat diffusion. In complete contrast, organic materials such as concrete and stone are also prominent elements in modern home design.

Many of the increasingly sophisticated innovations in kitchens and bathrooms are the result of technological developments. The phrase 'ambient intelligence' has been coined to describe the way we can now control many elements of the home – heating, lighting, sound, vision and much more – through automation. Home technology is the fastest-developing field of any covered in this book, and the one with the most far-reaching consequences for the consumer. Improvements are designed not only to make our lives easier but also to minimize damage to the environment.

Jack Mama, creative director at Philips Design, is at the cutting-edge of these new developments. Mama worked on the Wake-up Light, an alarm clock that uses light rather than noise to rouse a sleeping person. He is now looking at ways to promote well-being by responding to our emotions and feelings. Some people are rebelling against the tyranny of technology, for example, and it is now fashionable for weekend retreats to be completely void of technological equipment, providing the perfect 'no-tech' break for stressed executives.

New technology has also changed the way we illuminate domestic spaces. Lighting has become increasingly sophisticated and more efficient in terms of its consumption of energy and materials. Incandescent lightbulbs are being phased out and replaced by more eco-friendly alternatives. Products such as compact fluorescent lights (CFLs), light-emitting diodes (LEDs), fibre optics and electroluminescent materials have enabled designers to 'draw' with light, using a wide range of colours.

Gregorio Spini, founder of the Italian lighting company Kundalini, believes that LED technology is shaping the thinking of lighting designers, especially in the context of architectural lighting. LEDs, usually used to light small areas, and the recently developed high-voltage LEDs, which give much more light, are providing many new opportunities. While much contemporary lighting in the home is designed to be concealed, sculptural lighting features such as the extraordinary chandeliers of Ingo Maurer and the pink-neon Tree Light by Front Design are also highly prized.

Fibre-optic lighting made of transparent plastic, glass or a combination of the two is being taken to increasingly sophisticated lengths. Fibre optics' flexibility and colour spectrum allows designers to sculpt or weave with colour, producing futuristic designs such as Nox, an elegant pendant light by Refer and Staer.

Such is the flexibility of LEDs that they can also be incorporated as decorative elements in wall and floor coverings. Luminoso, designed by Esti Barnes for Top Floor, is a wool rug inset with LEDs in many colours, resembling a constellation; while Terra Maestricht by Royal Mosa is a collection of ceramic floor and wall tiles with LEDs embedded in their surface.

In recent years, there has been a renaissance in highly decorated domestic interiors, though many designers believe that this trend is beginning to wane and being replaced by a more considered approach. Wall and floor coverings, perhaps more than any of the other interior details considered in this book, have been most dramatically affected by advances in technology. As shown in chapter one, computer-aided design and digital printing have opened up new possibilities for ingenuity and creativity in these areas. By contrast, we have also included exquisite reissued hand-printed Arts and Crafts wallpapers by Watts of Westminster, the grand decorating house established in 1874, which is still in business today.

Less seductive and often undervalued interior details such as doors, windows, staircases and radiators are also reviewed. Radiator design – which, until recently, was dominated by dull, white, flat-steel rectangles – is one of the least explored aspects of product design for interiors. Underfloor heating is becoming commonplace in new builds, but we have concentrated here, for the obvious reason of visibility, on sculptural radiators. As our homes become more energy-efficient, we will need fewer radiators, providing more opportunity to invest in fewer, better-designed statement pieces. Paul Priestman, a founder of the award-winning consultancy Priestman Goode, who is featured at the beginning of chapter three, set a precedent for innovation by designing Hot Spring, a simple vertical coil of bright steel. His main advice to those buying a radiator is to opt for a design that seems set to endure.

Thermally efficient products, which keep heat in or out in the most effective way, are an increasing priority for glass manufacturers. Innovations in this area also include self-cleaning glass, extra-strong glass and products such as the SGG PRIVA-LITE by Saint Gobain, which allows the transformation of glass from clear to opaque at the touch of a button.

There is a broad consensus among designers and architects that the design aesthetic of the future will be influenced at every turn by concerns about the environment and sustainability. Design for design's sake is a thing of the past and there is an increasing demand for products that will last. Casper Vissers, co-founder with Marcel Wanders of Moooi, the company responsible for such distinctive pieces as the monumental Horse Lamp, says simply, 'We've had art. We've had design. And now it's craft.' He reflects on the evolution of recent interior styles 'from minimalism to romance to sophistication'. It seems that minimalism is finally waning and floral prints are less popular than they were; instead, there is a return to more organic design and colours.

In the years since the design boom of the 1990s, consumers have developed an ever more discerning eye for design. We are prepared and willing to pay more for individual pieces. This is helping to elevate the value of hand-crafted items. Could it be that these are the ideal products of the future? Designer–makers are, after all, able to adapt easily to change – and, as the barriers between art, craft and design continue to break down, their work is already a presence in many of our homes. In general, craft-based industries are environmentally friendly in terms of locally sourced materials and means of manufacture, and they have a lasting appeal. They feed our demand for originality and our need for enduring quality.

Chapter one

WALLS AND FLOORS

→

Marcel Wanders

Marcel Wanders is an internationally renowned Dutch designer, one of the key figures of his generation, who has a remarkable ability to transform the ordinary into the extraordinary. Wanders's work in the 1990s drew a clear line between the starkness of modernism and the return of a more experimental aesthetic featuring form and pattern. Although only in his mid-forties, Wanders has already had a prolific output – from industrial, product and consumer design, to fashion and interior design and, most recently, architecture. He works with many of Europe's leading contemporary design firms, including B&B, Boffi, Bisazza, Poliform, Moroso, Flos, Cappellini, Droog Design, Magis and Moooi. He also runs his own eponymously named studio in Amsterdam.

Known worldwide for his unpredictable, quirky and totally original forms of self-expression, Wanders enjoys blurring boundaries and revivifying familiar domestic forms, using new materials and techniques to express new ideas. His work is displayed in museums and galleries around the world, from the Museum of Modern Art in New York to the Victoria and Albert Museum in London.

Wanders's first step into the limelight was as one of the early members of Droog Design, founded in 1993 by Gijs Bakker and Renny Ramakers. Here he designed the product that first brought him to public attention – Knotted Chair, which is still produced today by Cappellini. In 2000, Wanders co-founded with Casper Vissers the radical Dutch design company Moooi; Wanders remains creative director, though Cappellini now own 50 per cent of the company. (Incidentally, the word 'moooi' is a misspelling of the Dutch word for beauty with an additional 'o' to imply added beauty – and beauty is Wanders's ultimate goal.) His great achievement is to have freed designers from the strictures of modernism, allowing them to experiment and to inject a wide variety of form and pattern into contemporary interiors.

In the course of his career, Wanders has designed countless wall and floor coverings. Apart from his work for Moooi, he has designed, for example, mosaics for Bisazza, carpets for Colorline and Linoleum for Forbo. He recently designed a wallpaper collection for the British company Graham & Brown; the Couture range mixes matts with metallics and features a bold geometric repeat pattern that echoes the petrified lace seen in Wanders's furniture pieces – blurring, as Wanders is fond of doing, the boundaries between different elements of design.

'More important than what we did for Graham & Brown is why we did it,' says Wanders. 'We are working towards a deeper level of understanding and a deeper level of beauty.' Wanders sees his role as a designer in clearly defined terms. 'I'm on a mission to redress the mistakes we've made for probably a hundred years. We've tried to make life simpler; we've tried to make production simpler; we've tried to be rational about everything – and we've pretty much succeeded in it. And I want to make sure that we don't have to live in a world that is super-rationalized, where everything can be taken away because it doesn't make sense any more. As a designer, you have to go beyond what is reasonable in beauty and give the best you can give.'

Wanders is particularly concerned about the status of design. 'We used to think of designers as representing a universal newness – as this super-intelligent group of people who would speak the truth,' he says. 'In fact, over the years, the design world has become obsessed by style, more preoccupied by the dogmatic interpretation of an old idea than with cultivating a free spirit. I think that, over the last ten years, design has learned to be more than it was; it is not searching for honesty as much as for a personalized kind of poetry. We have been able implement new ideas on beauty and find other directions for expression.' Wanders also believes that today's designers have a lot to learn from the past and a lot to give to the future. 'Now we have shown ourselves to be revolutionary,' he says, 'we try to be evolutionary. Durability has always been key in my work, and I believe that the ecological challenges that face us today are psychological. If people don't like something, they throw it away because it doesn't satisfy their need for newness any more. This is because we have made the new so important in our culture. We must start to make the old as valuable as the new in the popular imagination. I want to make things that are not too new to start with. We think that timeless design is the modern style, which is not true. There are things designed in the 1950s and 1960s that look completely old-fashioned now, and there are things that may be a hundred years old that haven't lost any quality. If you try to be very modern, you will soon be very old-fashioned. If you want to make durable stuff, don't make modern stuff. You cannot make a durable world if you don't show appreciation of the past.'

Wanders has strong views about the meaning of inspiration. 'More and more people think they are inspired because they open a book to find a picture they like and they can make a drawing from it. The true meaning of the word inspiration is about people with a divine fire burning in them, people with a mission and a purpose in life. I am not inspired simply by the colour red or by some guy who makes nice objects. I really want to make this earth a bit different, to make design truly more romantic, truly more durable, truly more meaningful to my surroundings.'

Bonaparte by Carlo Dal Bianco for Bisazza. Decorative mosaic panel, representation of Canova's sculptures using 10 x 10mm (½ x ½in) tesserae. Panel size: (H) 2905 x (W) 1300mm (114 x 51in). www.bisazza.com

←

Pinocchio rug by Hayshop. From the Hay carpet collection. 100 % pure knotted wool. Multicoloured, random design, making each rug individual. (Diameter) 900 or 1400cm (35½ or 55in). www.hayshop.dk

↑
Winter-Flowers-Oro-Bianco by Carlo Dal
Bianco for the Bisazza
Decori 20 collection.
Mosaic tesserae made of a
24kt gold leaf sandwiched
between two protective
layers of glass. Panel size:
(H) 2912 x (W) 1294mm
(115 x 51in).
www.bisazza.com

↑
Leopardo by Carlo Dal
Bianco from the Urban
Safari collection for
Bisazza. Venetian enamel
mosaic of square tesserae.
Panel size: (H) 966 x
(W) 966mm (38 x 38in).
www.bisazza.com

→

Red Oak flooring from the Dark Classic range by Amtico. Sizes: 76 x 915; 114 x 915; 152 x 915mm (3 x 36; 4½ x 36; 6 x 36in). www.amtico.com

↓ →

Plynyl tile by Chilewich. Woven vinyl fabric bonded to heavy-duty vinyl backing reinforced with non-woven ceramic mesh; can be laid in any pattern desired. Various wood-grain finishes available. Tiles: 457 x 457mm (18 x 18in). www.chilewich.com

→
Polar Glass Arctic (smooth) from the Polar Glass collection by Amtico. Glass tiles in silver or blue with smooth or bevelled finish. 305 x 305mm (12 x 12in). www.amtico.com

↓
Koffe Fineline by Formica Veneer. Reconstituted wood including poplar, obeche, basswood and bamboo. Various colours and wax or polyurethane finish. 3050 x 1300mm (120 x 51in). www.formica.co.uk

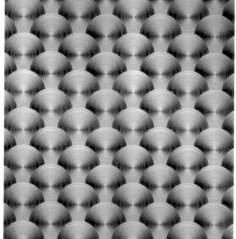

←
Apollo from the Formica Metallics collection by Formica. Laminate composed of metal foils. Various other finishes available from a mirror-like polish to embossed and burnished metals. 2440 x 1020mm (96 x 40in). www.formica.co.uk

←

Nuolja from the Ethnic collection by Bolon. Woven-vinyl floor covering, slip-resistant, sound-absorbing, does not fray. Roll size: 25 x 2m (82 x 6½ft). www.bolon.se

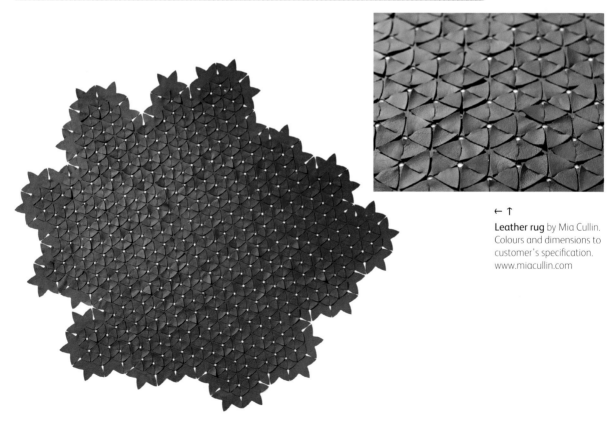

← ↑

Leather rug by Mia Cullin. Colours and dimensions to customer's specification. www.miacullin.com

→ **Four Leaf Clover** leather rug by Mia Cullin. Colours and dimensions to customer's specification. www.miacullin.com

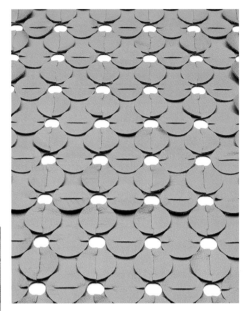

← **Velvet tiles** from the New Baroque collection by Settecento studio. Range of plain and patterned tiles in porcelain stoneware with shiny surface, available in a variety of colours including green/brown (illustrated here). 24 x 72cm or 11.9 x 72cm (9½ x 28in or 4½ x 28in). www.settecento.com

← **Concreate** wall and floor tiles by Rex Ceramiche Artistiche. Range of square, rectangular and mosaic tiles in porcelain. Available in a variety of colours including Mud, illustrated. 450 x 450mm (18 x 18in). www.rex-cerart.com

→

Doodle wall designed by Linda Florence. Panels screenprinted by hand with iron filings and flock. Grey and white.
2 x 4m (6½ x 13ft).
www.lindaflorence.co.uk

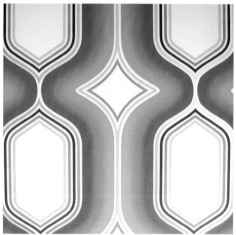

← ↑

Boheme from the Drama collection, updated design from Graham & Brown wallpaper archive. Shown above in orange with a touch of metallic. Also available in green or black. Roll size: 10 x 0.52m (32 x 1½ft).
www.grahambrown.com

↓
Grey Birdseye rug by Orla
Kiely. 100 % tufted wool,
also available in yellow.
Two sizes: 1200 x 1800
and 2400 x 3000mm
(47 x 71 and 94 x 118in).
www.orlakiely.com

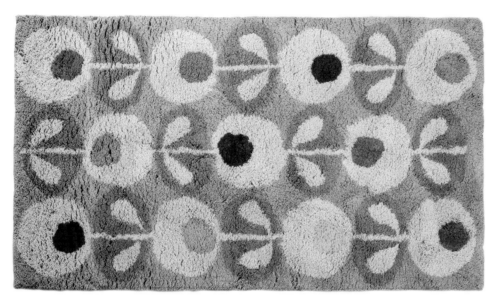

↓
In The Woods rug by
Michaela Schleypen.
100 % New Zealand wool.
Grey/brown, beige/brown,
charcoal, dark brown.
Original size: 900 x 2500
or 2000 x 2000mm
(35½ x 98 or 79 x 79in),
but can be made to any
size and shape.
www.floortoheaven.com

↓

Kho Liang le Collection
by Royal Mosa Maastricht.
Reissued tiles, originally
designed in the 1960s.
Gloss white. Relief designs
include circles, segments
of circles, diagonals
and triangles.
100 x 100mm (4 x 4in).
www.royalmosa.com

→

Powder designed by
Andre Putman, part of
the BrixSystem for Surface
Tiles. Porcelain tiles with
random shading. Available
in grey, avana (sand)
and dark in various size
formats. Square tile: 594 x
594mm (23½ x 23½in).
www.surfacetiles.com

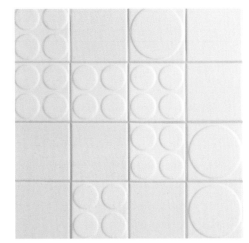

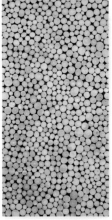

← ↑

Twig wall panel by
Pinch Design. Ash forest
thinnings. (H) 2440 x
(W) 1220 x (D) 60mm
(96 x 48 x 2½in), but
can be made to order.
www.pinchdesign.com

←

Leaf Metallic wallpaper by
Jocelyn Warner. Available
in silver/grey, black/gold
or turquoise/gold (shown
here). Roll size: 10.05 x
0.52m (33 x 1½ft).
www.jocelynwarner.com

→

Do You Live in a Town?
wallpaper by Absolute Zero
Degrees for Minimoderns.
Milk chocolate only.
Roll size: 10 x 0.52m
(33 x 1½ft).
www.minimoderns.com

←

Tick-Tock wallpaper by Absolute Zero Degrees for Minimoderns. Shown here in Snow. 'Colour-Me' print designed to be coloured in once hung. Roll size: 10 x 0.52m (32 x 1½ft). www.minimoderns.com

←

Esquire rug by Esti Barnes for Top Floor. Hand-tufted New Zealand wool pile, backing cotton, mesh and latex. Any size, any colour. www.topfloorrugs.com

↑

Mystery by Michaela Schleypen from the Floor Couture collection. Custom-made rug in 100 % New Zealand wool. Any colour. Original size 1700 x 2400mm (66 x 94in), but can be made to any size or shape. www.floortoheaven.com

←

Stitched silk wallpaper
by Claire Coles. Traditional
wallpaper motifs machine-
embroidered onto silk
wallpaper. Teal and black.
(W) 0.55 x (L) 3m
(21½ x 118in).
www.clairecoles
design.co.uk

← ↑

Rug Silver Leaves by
Michaela Schleypen.
100 % specially twisted
New Zealand wool. Pattern
highlights are made of
shiny, soft, viscose-coated
metal fibre. Original size
2000 x 2000mm (79 x
79in) but can be custom-
made to any shape or size.
www.floortoheaven.com

→

Hybride carpet from
Revanche Collection
designed by Emmanuelle
Payard for Tai Ping. Jute,
cotton and spun silk mix
in bleached white. Made
to order.
www.taipingcarpets.com

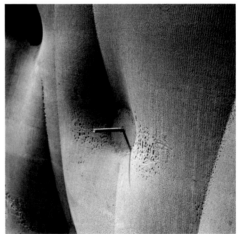

←

Amicia Honeybird
wallpaper by Watts of
Westminster. Hand-printed
design. Colour as shown.
Wallpaper width:
460mm (18in).
www.wattsof
westminster.com

↑

Fabric Formed Concrete
by Scin. Engineered
geotextiles made from
durable synthetic polymers
or polypropylene allows
complete shapes in
concrete to be made.
Available in grey, white,
buffs and pinks dependent
upon sand specification.
www.scin.co.uk

←

Masonite boards by Chandra Ahlsell and Anna Holmquist for Folkform. Wood-fibre pressed with organic materials. 1220 x 2440mm (48 x 96in). www.folkform.se

↓

Camberwell wallpaper by Watts of Westminster. Hand-printed design drawn from a fragment of wallpaper attributed to C. F. A. Voysey. Colours red or Iona. Wallpaper width: 520mm (20½in). www.wattsof westminster.com

←

Fossil Leaves decorative panel by Futimis. Heat-pressed Ecoresin. One of many designs. (W) 1220 x (L) 2440mm (48 x 96in). www.futimis-systems.com

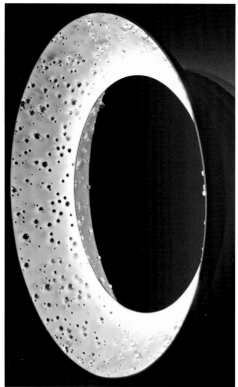

↑

Eclipse mirror by Bodo
Sperlein. Frame made
from thermoformed
DuPont Corian in pure
glacier white. Multiple
colour options available.
Set with approximately
500 Swarovski crystals.
Frame backlit using Phillips
T5 lighting technology.
Large: (Diameter) 1000 x
(D) 300mm (39½ x 12in).
Medium: (Diameter) 800 x
(D) 200mm (31½ x 8in).
www.bodosperlein.co.uk

→

Luminoso by Esti Barnes
for Top Floor. Hand-tufted
100 % New Zealand wool.
Interwoven with LEDS on
cotton backing. Custom
designed in any size,
design or colourway.
www.topfloorrugs.com

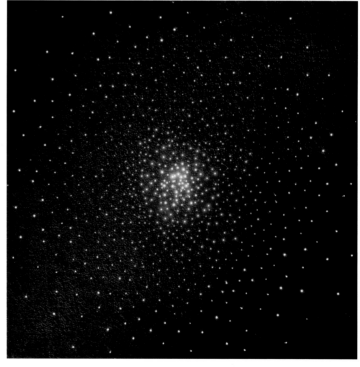

↑ →

French Dot by Nama Rococo from the Couture range for Nama Rococo wallpaper studio. Wallpaper, partly hand-painted on acid-free French paper. Colour: Ooh La black. Sold by the single sheet: 965 x 635mm (38 x 25in). www.namarococo.com

→

D Spin rug by Paula Lenti. Handmade wool rope available in seven different shades. (W) 1400 x (L) 3150mm (55 x 124in). www.paolalenti.com

↑

Kitchen appliance tiles by Alice Mara. Spanish earthenware, digitally printed with black and white imagery of kitchen appliances. 100 x 100mm (4 x 4in). www.alicemara.com

→

Slide shelving unit by Simon Pengelly for Modus. Series of boxes, each able to slide to the left or right, depending on requirements. White lacquered MDF. (H) 2040 x (W) 816–1250 x (D) 287mm (80 x 32–49 x 11in). www.modusfurniture.co.uk

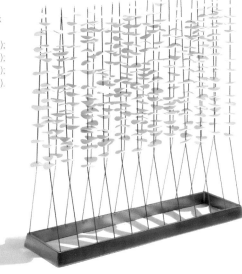

←

Zaha Hadid rug from the Hope by Designers collection for Arzu rugs. 100 % wool, individually hand-knotted in a Nooristan weave in black and white. Four sizes: 86 x 312cm (34 x 123in); 94 x 310cm (37 x 122in); 89 x 417cm (35 x 164in); 91 x 366cm (36 x 144in). www.arzurugs.org

↑

Forest room divider designed by Monica Forster for Modus. Stainless steel, MDF-lacquered and die-cut 100 % pure new wool felt. (H) 630 x (W) 330 x (D) 200mm (25 x 13 x 8in) or (H) 930 x (W) 330 x (D) 1030mm (36½ x 13 x 40½in). www.modusfurniture.co.uk

↓

Crosto Bianco by Rex Ceramiche Artistiche, from the Metrowall collection. White porcelain tiles. 304 x 608mm (12 x 24in). www.rexceramica.com

→

Little Field of Flowers
by Tord Boontje for
Nanimarquina. Hand-
loomed wool. Six
distinct shapes of flower
combinations in red,
green or grey. 800 x
1400mm (31½ x 55in),
1700 x 2400mm (67 x
94in) or 2000 x 3000mm
(79 x 118in).
www.nanimarquina.com

← ↑

Birds by Ed Annink for
Driade. Hand-tufted rug
in pure virgin wool.
(W) 2000 x (L) 3000mm
(79 x 118in).
www.driade.com

←

Abisko Le Rythme de L'Ombre Betulla Inserto Acciaio tiles by Maria Luisa Brighenti for Rex Ceramiche Artistiche. Fine porcelains with etched glass inlays for backlighting. 600 x 600mm (24 x 24in). www.rexceramica.com

↓

Kew wallpaper by Jocelyn Warner. Large-scale design taken from botanical drawings using gloss inks. Available in brown/blue, grey/gloss, cream/gold, black/gloss, turquoise/red. Roll size: 10.05 x 0.68m (33 x 2ft). www.jocelynwarner.com

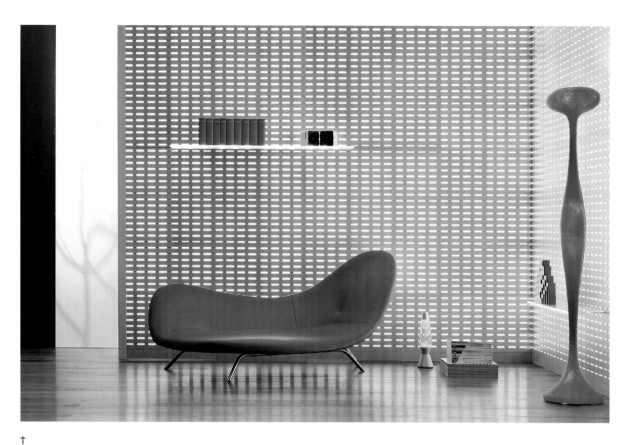

↑

Luminoso by Massimo
Iosa Ghini from the
Boiserie collection for
Listone Giordano. Wall
cladding in shaped,
moulded European maple
(5mm thick) supported by
aluminium frame.
Module: 1200 x 1000mm
(47 x 39½in).
www.listonegiordano.com

←

Braille wall flats by
Inhabit. Modular
embossed paper panels
designed to expand in any
direction, with peel-and-
stick adhesive tape and
automatic pattern repeat.
100 % moulded bamboo
pulp. Each panel: 457 x
457mm (18 x 18in).
www.inhabitliving.com

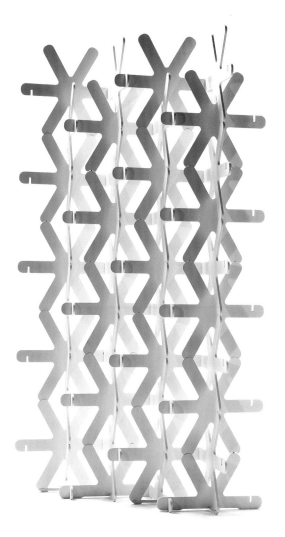

←

Yuki (snowflake) screen
by Nendo for Cappellini.
Plastic material (ABS)
composed of interlocking
and repeated forms. Black
or white. (H) 1810 x
(W) 1000 x (D) 305mm
(71 x 39½ x 12in).
www.cappellini.it

↓

Opus Incertum by Sean
Yoo for Casamania.
Multipurpose design;
can be used as partition,
display cabinet or
bookshelf. Expanded
polypropylene. Black, grey,
orange, white or gold.
(H) 1000 x (W) 1000 x
(D) 350mm (39½ x
39½ x 14in).
www.casamania.it

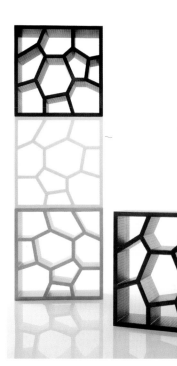

→

Geoblack by Eric Barrett
for Concrete Blond.
Concrete panels made
of recycled glass and
pulverized fuel ash from
power stations and blast
furnaces. Each panel:
(H) 1000 x (W) 1000 x
(D) 35mm
(39½ x 39½ x 1½in).
www.concrete-blond.com

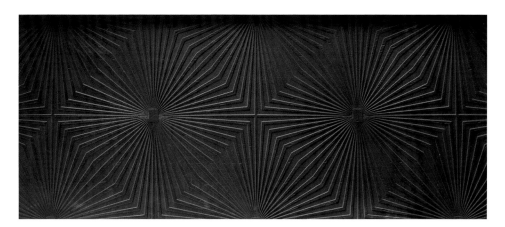

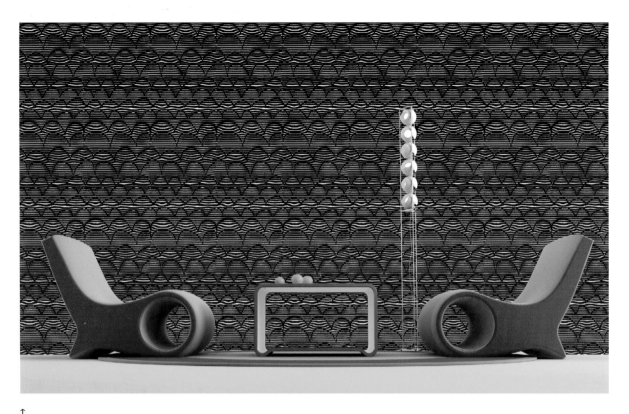

↑

Harmony in Caviar
wallpaper by Dominic
Crinson from the Ensemble
collection. Woven
wallpaper made from
textile fibres and cellulose.
Colours: slate, caviar or
fuchsia. Roll size: 5 x 0.46m
(16 x 1½ft).
www.crinson.com

←

Quartet wall tiles by
Dominic Crinson from the
Ensemble collection. Semi-
matt ceramic tiles, rectified
for seamless construction.
Available in porcelain for
floors. 200 x 200 (8 x 8in)
or 400 x 400mm
(16 x 16in).
www.crinson.com

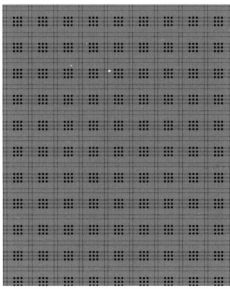

←

**Faster Rosa (Aunty
Rosa)** wallpaper by Lisa
Bengtsson from the Family
collection. Available in pink
or yellow. Bespoke digitally
printed design, made to
measure.
www.lisabengtsson.se

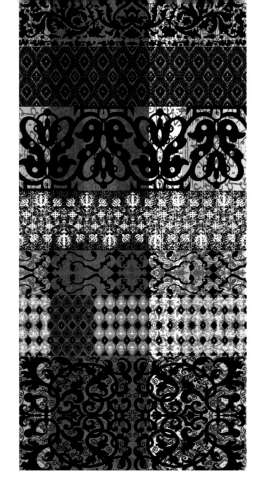

→

World Carpets collection
by Studio Marcel Wanders
for Colorline. Customize
you own carpet. Choose
from seven different
patterns and seventeen
colours. Pattern can be
printed onto several
types and qualities of
broadloom, 4000mm
(157in) wide. Minimum
quantity 100 sq m
(1076 sq ft).
www.colorline.nl

←

Light-emitting wallpaper
by Jonas Samson.
Wallpaper combined
with electroluminescent
material. Special driver
supplied connects to
normal electric socket so
design may be turned on
and off. Shapes, colours,
fades and primitive
animations to order.
Maximum size sheet:
3 x 1.5m (10 x 5ft).
www.jonassamson.com

→
Thistle rug by Timorous
Beasties. Red, cream,
stone or earth. 100 % New
Zealand wool. (W) 1900 x
(L) 2950mm (75 x 116in).
www.timorousbeasties.com

↑
Iguana wallpaper by
Timorous Beasties from the
Superwide collection. Black,
grey, silver and white on
Ivory. Sold per metre.
(W) 1350mm (53in).
www.timorousbeasties.com

→
Grace Wallpaper and
Flourishes from the 'ready
to wear' collection by
Catherine Hammerton.
Customized wallpaper
can be hung five different
ways. Decorative details
(for Flourishes) are added
separately. Surface printed
and embossed in Chantilly
cream. Grace wallpaper:
Roll size: 10 x 0.52m
(32 x 1½ft). Grace
Flourishes: five A4 sheets.
www.catherine
hammerton.com

↓ →

Vider Mint by Jan Meerdink for Winoldi. Flexible room divider, handmade. Transparent silicone woven with silver anodized aluminium strips. Other designs available. Standard size: 2200 x 1800mm (87 x 71in); can be rolled into 200mm (8in) pillar. Other sizes on request.
www.winoldi.com

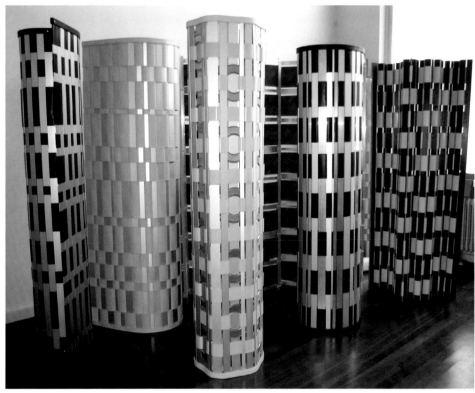

←

Flute screens by Giles Miller of Farm Designs. Corrugated cardboard. (H) 1700 x (W) 1200 x 400mm (67 x 47 x 16in).
www.farmdesigns.co.uk

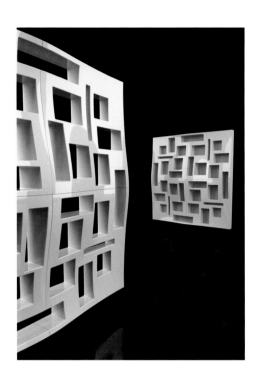

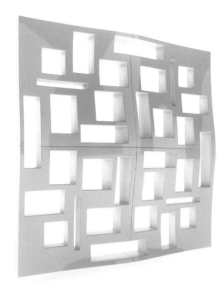

←

Trilli bookcase by Marino Rossato for Kappaventotto. Suspended wall units in polyurethane foam, lacquered gloss white. Backs to shelves optional but available in six contrasting colours. Units can be used singly or as a group. (H) 900 x (W) 900 x (D) 240mm (35½ x 35½ x 9½in). www.k28italia.it

↓

Molo Softwall by Stephanie Forsythe and Todd MacAllen of Molo Design. Lightweight, free-standing partition made from a flexible honeycomb paper structure. Available in two types of paper in black, white or brown. Expands from less than 50mm (2in) to just over 6m (19½ft) in length. www.molodesign.com

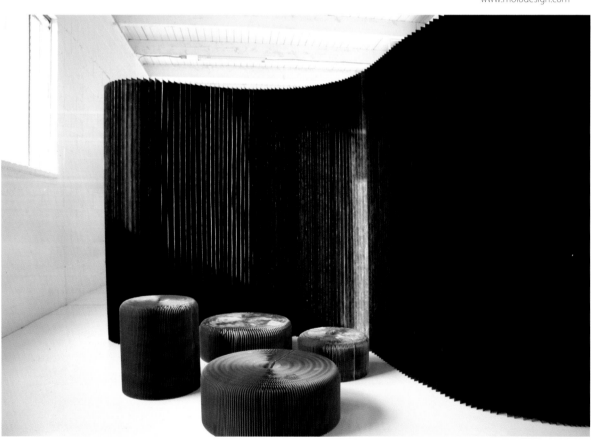

←
Snowflake by Studio
Marcel Wanders and
Bisazza. Ceramic mosaic
with computer-generated
design in whites and greys.
Composed of 10mm (½in)
glass mosaics.
www.bisazza.it

↓
Pretty Big Wall by Afroditi
Krassa from the Divine
collection. Mirror, polished
stainless steel, suspended
on polypropylene rope.
(H) 2200 x (W) 340mm
(87 x 13½in).
www.afroditi.com

↑
Re-Deco by Jaime Hayon
for Lladro from the
Re-Deco collection. Oval
mirror. Porcelain with glass
and platinum lustre.
(H) 1640 x (W) 1600mm
(64 x 63in).
www.lladro.com

↑

Porcelain tiles from the Matouche collection emulate various organic textures such as Croco (crocodile) illustrated. Elephant, reptile and distressed leather also available in black, brown and ivory. Tiles 610 x 610mm (24 x 24in). www.walkerzanger.com

→

Hagga rug by Gunilla Lagerhem Ullberg. Shaft-woven hair-yarn rug 100 % wool woven on linen warp. (W) 850, 1350, 1650, 1950, 2450 or 3400mm (33, 53, 65, 77, 96 or 134in). www.kasthall.com

→

Ginza rug by Helen Yardley. Pure Jacob's sheep natural wool yarn. Cut pile/loop hand-tufted. Colour as shown. (W) 1750 x (L) 2200mm (69 x 87in). www.helenyardley.com

↓

Puzzlefloor by Niagara for Puzzlefloor. Wooden tiles in two different patterns custom-made to fit room. Available in thirteen colours. Made of solid tongue and groove northern hardwood, each piece pre-finished and precision-cut. www.puzzlefloor.com

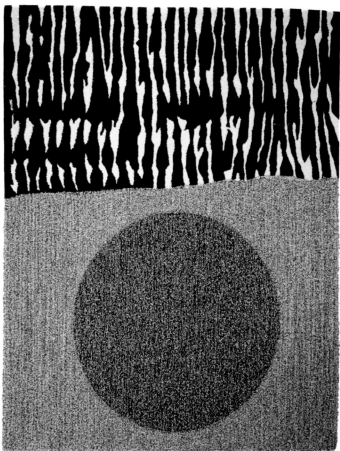

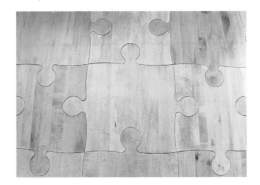

←

Wooden carpet by Christian Anderegg for Anderegg AG, Ulisbach. 6mm-thick hardwood combined with flexible adhesive. Non-slip, reversible, oiled for protection. Various dimensions. www.aak-ideen.ch

→

Naxos X-wall Square
by Naxos. Handcrafted
ceramic room divider.
(H) 3000–3100mm
(118–122in).
www.naxos-ceramica.it

→

**Moooi carpet model
01** by Marcel Wanders
for Moooi. Printed nylon
threads, white with blue
patterns. Other versions
available. (Diameter)
2500mm (98in).
www.moooi-online.com

Poodle wallpaper by Wonderwalls, specialists in original and limited-edition designs. Made-to-measure wallpaper design. Size, style and colours customized to request. www.wonder-walls.net

→

Moooi carpet model **05** by Marcel Wanders for Moooi. Printed nylon threads in black and white. 2500 x 2500mm (98 x 98in). www.moooi-online.com

←

Moooi carpet model 04 by Marcel Wanders for Moooi. Printed nylon threads. 2000 x 3000mm (79 x 118in). www.moooi-online.com

↑

Bloom stair runner by
Rebecca von Gyer. Shown
here in crimson. Also
available in iris or cocoa.
Hand-tufted 100 %
New Zealand wool.
Made to measure.
www.gyer.co.uk

↓

I Love Me by Ich&Kar
for Domestic. Laser-cut
Perspex mirror. (H) 500 x
(W) 500 x (D) 3mm
(20 x 20 x ¼in).
www.domestic.fr

→

Spline by Matali Crasset
for Domestic. Laser-cut
Perspex mirror. (H) 1000 x
(W) 500 x (D) 3mm
(40 x 20 x ¼in).
www.domestic.fr

↓
Manhattan Skyline
wallpaper by Wonderwalls,
specialists in one-off and
limited-edition wallpapers.
Size, style and colours
customized to request.
www.wonder-walls.net

←
Rouge by Rebecca von
Gyer. Hand-tufted 100 %
New Zealand wool rug.
Also in black and white.
Made to measure.
www.gyer.co.uk

→
Fleur by Rebecca von Gyer.
Hand-tufted 100 % New
Zealand wool rug. Made
to measure.
www.gyer.co.uk

→

Message in a Box by Wendy Plomp (detail). Carpet made of recycled cardboard. Various colours and patterns. (W) 900 or 1000 x (L) 800 or 2000mm (35½ or 39 x 31½ or 79in).
www.wnd.nu

↓

Family by Lisa Bengtsson for Wonderwalls. Interactive wallpaper that provides an alternative way to mount family photos. Black and white. Roll size: 10 x 0.53m (32 x 1½ft).
www.wonder-walls.net

↑

Blow Up by Fratelli Campana of the Campana Brothers for Alessi. Wall mirror part of the Blow Up collection. Stainless steel, mirror. (H) 745 x (W) 865 x (D) 110mm (29 x 34 x 4in).
www.alessi.com

→

Warping wallpaper
by Tom Hanke for
Surrealien. Individually
generated wallpaper
based on detailed plans
of your walls, creating
effects around existing
fixtures. Fleece wallpaper.
Maximum wall height
7.5m (24½ft).
www.surrealien.de

↓

Jacobean wallpaper in
charcoal by Celia Birtwell.
Roll length: 10m (32ft).
www.celiabirtwell.com

↑

Peacock wall panel
by Helen Amy Murray.
Handmade appliqué in
Novasuede and wadding.
Can be made in many
materials, colours and
dimensions. Made to order.
www.helenamymurray.com

←

Oriental Orchid wallpaper by Timorous Beasties from the Studio collection. Roll size: 10 x 0.52m (32 x 1½ft). www.timorousbeasties.com

↑

Bloom rug by Jocelyn Warner. 100 % hand-knotted wool. (W) 1830 x (L) 1830mm (72 x 72in). www.jocelynwarner.com

↑

Homes illustrated wallpaper by Erica Wakerly. Available in black/cream or brown/cream. Roll size: 10 x 0.52m (32 x 1½ft). www.printpattern.com

←
BTV Stampede wallpaper
by Beyond the Valley.
Viewed as abstract
pattern from distance.
Dark chocolate and cream.
Roll size: 10 x 0.52m
(32 x 1½ft).
www.beyondthevalley.com

←
Leaf wall panel by Anne
Kyyro Quinn. Sound-
absorbing panel. 100 %
wool felt, outer layer
twisted creating a 3D
effect. Available in twenty-
five colours. Dimensions to
client specification.
www.annekyyroquinn.com

↓
Forest wallpaper by Peng
Creative for Rollout.
Latex-based, digitally
printed inkjet wallpaper.
Custom-made. Can be
printed to required size.
www.rollout.ca

←

mohohej! DIA by
Michal Kopaniszyn and
Magdalena Lubinska for
Moho Design. Pattern
makes reference to
Polish folk-art paper cuts.
100 % pure wool. Various
colours. (Diameter) 1100
or 1800mm (43 or 71in).
Other sizes on request.
www.mohodesign.com

↓ →

Moon screen by Carlo
Ballabio for Emmemobili.
Oak with lacquer finish.
Various colours. (H) 1800 x
(W) 2400mm (71 x 94in).
www.emmemobili.it

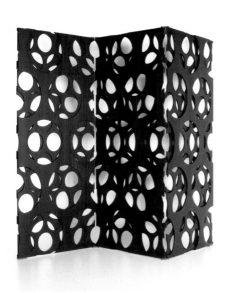

↑

Deer Antler by Sibylle Pfeiffer for Pulpo. Double hook/holder. Powder-coated steel available in ten colours. Conforms to standard European tile sizes and can be combined with ceramic tiles designs or with adapter attached to any wall. 150 x 150mm (6 x 6in). www.cmdag.ch

↑

Floris by Klaartje Daamen for Tom Frencken. Modular flooring system composed of MDF and cardboard sandwich panel with 3mm walnut veneer. Tiles are 400 x 400mm (16 x 16in) and come in a variety of depths: 50, 250 or 450mm (2, 10 or 18in). They can be used to make integral chairs, tables and so on. www.tomfrencken.nl

↑

Miles by Big-game design studio. Hand-tufted wool rug. Red, blue or grey. Comes with three wooden toy cars. (W) 1500 x (L) 1000mm (59 x 39in). www.balouga.com

→

Lace cast-concrete floor tiles by Jethro Macey. For exterior or interior use. Available in white, grey and charcoal. Each batch is handmade to order. Interior tiles: (W) 300 x (L) 300 x (D) 15mm (12 x 12 x ½in). Exterior tiles: (W) 300 x (L) 300 x (D) 30mm (12 x 12 x 1in). www.jethromacey.com

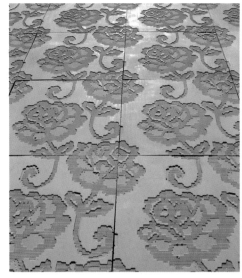

↓

Black and White Forest mural by Nic Miller. From the Photography collection by Surface Design from the Victoria and Albert Museum photo library. Over 140 images to choose from. www.surfaceview.co.uk

↑

Walled paper by Eric Barrett of Concrete Blond. Textured and patterned concrete castings in a variety of sizes, finishes and patterns. www.concrete-blond.com

← Svärmor (mother-in-law) wallpaper by Lisa Bengtsson from the Family range. Black and white. Roll size: 10 x 0.52m (32 x 1½ft). www.lisabengtsson.se

↓ Big Tulip Print wallpaper by Orla Kiely. Olive. Roll size: 10 x 0.52m (32 x 1½ft). www.orlakiely.com

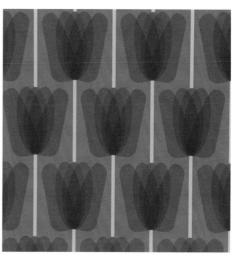

← Mural Flower heads by Nic Miller from the Photography collection by Surface Design. Photo illustration from the Victoria and Albert Museum photo library. Over 140 images to choose from. www.surfaceview.co.uk

→

Sunshine rug by Pacha Mama. Leather, available in orange (shown), beige, bronze or gold. (Diameter) 2420mm (95in). www.pacha-mama.net

↑

Modanato by Massimo Iosa Ghini from the Boiseries collection. Modular wall cladding, moulded wenge or white Montblanc oak. Modules available in three sizes: 1200 x 1200mm (47 x 47in), 1200 x 900mm (47 x 35½in) or 1200 x 700mm (47 x 27½in). www.listonegiordano.com

↑

Farfar (Grandpa) by Lisa Bengtsson from the Family range. Digitally printed made-to-measure bespoke wallpaper. www.lisabengtsson.se

←

Bodywall Silhouette
by Dominic Crinson.
Digitally printed mural
tiles. Can also be printed
on wallpaper. Various
dimensions: 200 x 200,
200 x 300 or 280 x
400mm (8 x 8, 8 x 12
or 11 x 16in).
www.crinson.com

→

Manuscrit rug by Joaquim
Ruiz Millet from the Black
on White collection for
Nanimarquina. Based
on designer's own
handwriting. Handmade
and hand-tufted 100 %
New Zealand wool. 2000 x
3000, 1700 x 2400 or 800
x 2400mm (79 x 118,
67 x 94 or 31½ x 94in).
www.nanimarquina.com

→
Platina White tiles by Studio Marcel Wanders for Dutch Design Tiles. Ceramic wall and floor tiles, white, grey, black. Wall tiles: 148 x 148mm (6 x 6in). Floor tiles 198 x 198 or 300 x 300mm (8 x 8 or 12 x 12in). www.dutchdesigntiles.com

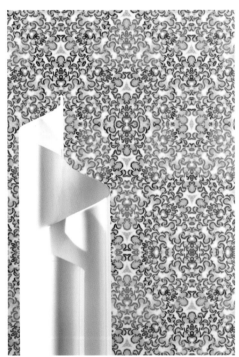

↑
Hokusai Wave by Dominic Crinson from the Extreme Collection of wallpapers. Non-woven wallpaper of textile fibres and cellulose. All wallpapers made to order. Roll size: 5 x 0.46m (16½ x 1½ft). www.crinson.com

→
Yee-Ha! by Paul Loebach for Studio Printworks. Hand-printed wallpaper available in twelve colourways. Wallpaper width: 686mm (27in). www.studioprintworks.com

→

X by Pippo Lionni for Ligne Roset. Hand-tufted rug in 100 % pure New Zealand wool. Dimensions and colours to customer's specification.
www.ligne-roset.co.uk

↓

Tred Reduction by Pippo Lionni for Wool Classics. Hand-tufted rug in 100 % pure New Zealand wool. Colours and dimensions to customer's specification.
www.woolclassics.com

→

Moooi carpet model 8 by Marcel Wanders for Moooi. Printed nylon threads. Brown, white, black. Other versions available. (W) 3000 x (L) 2000mm (118 x 79in).
www.moooi-online.com

→

LitraconT by Aron Losonczi for Litracon. Light-transmitting concrete – a combination of optical fibres and fine concrete. Building material for exterior and interior walls. Building blocks in max size: (H) 300 x (W) 600 x (D) 25–500mm (12 x 24 x 1–20in). www.litracon.hu

↓

Vetro Modular by Criterion Tiles from the Avant-garde range. Meshed-back mosaic of oxide-smelted opaque glass. Varying brick shapes with deep pearlescent glaze. Colours: bianco, avorio, silver tortora, cemento, moka, carbone. Sheet size: 250 x 210mm (10 x 8½in). www.criterion-tiles.co.uk

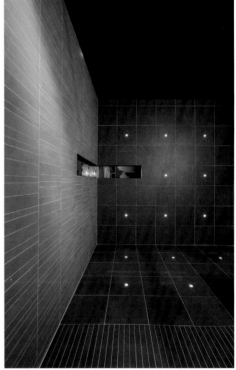

↑

Terra LED by Royal Mosa from the Terra Maestricht collection. Ceramic wall and floor tiles with integral LED lights. Grey, beige or brown. Tiles: 450 x 450mm or 600 x 600mm (18 x 18 or 24 x 24in). www.royalmosa.com

↑

**Leather floor and wall
tiles** by Edelman Leather.
European, full-grain,
vegetable-tanned, aniline-
dyed cowhide, develops
deep patina with age.
Illustrated: Smooth black
tile in Tromp L'oiel.
Various shapes, colours
and finishes available.
Tile size up to: (W) 475 x
(L) 475 x (D) 3–3.5mm
(19 x 19 x ¼in).
www.edelmanleather.com

↓

Memento rug by Ksenia
Movafagh for 2 Form
Design. Laser-cut pattern
8mm (½in) two-layer
woollen felt. Black or white.
Other colours available
to order. (W) 1700 x
(L) 2400mm (67 x 94in).
www.2form.no

→

Rose Lace rug by Kiki van
Eijk. Handmade in wool.
Shown here in grey and
white. (W) 1800 x
(L) 2780mm (71 x 109in).
Other colours and sizes
available on request.
www.kikiworld.nl

↑ →

Sloophout wallpaper by
Studio Ditte. Photographs
of scrap wood composed
around a dominating
colour: white, brown-
grey and green. Pattern
stretches out over 4.5m
(15ft). Roll size: 9 x 0.45m
(29½ x 1½ft).
www.designdailys.nl

→

Degre by Surface Tiles.
Part of the Brix system.
Porcelain tiles with random
shading. Available in grey,
avana (sand) and dark
in various size formats.
Square tile: 286 x 286mm
(11 x 11in).
www.surfacetiles.com

↑

Solid Poetry by Frederik
Molenschot and Susanne
Happle. Concrete tiles,
pattern only revealed
when surface wet or air
humid. Custom-made,
dimensions variable.
www.frederikmolenschot.nl

←

Silvergate by Farrow
& Ball. Block-printed
wallpaper from Special
Edition 1. Early nineteenth-
century English damask
paper originally printed
at Silvergate in Norfolk.
Coloured grounds
traditionally brush-applied
before the design is block-
printed. Roll size:
10 x 0.53m (32 x 1½ft).
www.farrow-ball.com

Daisy White by Carlo Dal Bianco from the Glass Tiles collection for Bisazza. Computer-aided design with glass chip mosaics and inlaid motifs, creating smooth level and seamless surface. Available in red, blue or white. Panels: (H) 600 x (W) 600mm (24 x 24in). www.bisazza.com

→

Info Paper by Christopher Pearson for Graham & Brown. Wallpaper featuring copy from a phrase book. Roll size: 10.58 x 0.52m (35 x 1½ft). www.grahambrown.com

↓

Flower by Hemingway Design. Floral tiles with light-reflective surface from the Wet range of large-scale ceramic tiles. Available in white, mink or natural. 198 x 248mm (8 x 10in). www.wettiles.co.uk

→

←

Toothbrush by Hemingway Design. Large-scale satin-finish ceramic tiles from the Wet range. Available in white/silver, mink/silver and black/silver. 398 x 248mm (15½ x 10in). www.wettiles.co.uk

↑

Elizabeth by Graham & Brown. Flock effect wallpaper. Shown here in pink/silver, also available in black/white, bronze/chocolate, chocolate/turquoise and chartreuse/chocolate. Roll size: 10 x 0.52m (32 x 1½ft). www.grahambrown.com

←

Eliot Rug (Large Circles) by Massimo Fenati for the Isos collection. Die-cut felt. Available in three designs, nine colours and three sizes. Large: (W) 2500 x (L) 1550mm (98 x 61in). www.isoscollection.co.uk

←

SAIL wall system by Paolo Bistacchi for Albed. Can be equipped with a range of accessories including sinks and basins. Aluminium and frosted glass, bleached oak. Various dimensions. www.albed.it

↑

Reflection mirror by Piero Lissoni for Porro. One of a collection of rectangular wall mirrors. Surrounds in painted metal and satinized bronze. Available in three sizes: 700 x 1800, 900 x 2300 or 2300 x 1800mm (27½ x 71, 35½ x 90½ or 90½ x 71in). www.porro.com

→

Corallo mosaic panel by Marco Brago for the Fresh collection for Bisazza. Coral, white and gold tesserae; colour as shown. Panel size: 2905 x 1291mm (114 x 51in). www.bisazza.com

← Wall-mounted three-dimensional textile by Fiona Zobole. Screen-printed, layered text, hand-printed onto canvas in neutral shades. Made to commission. Standard dimension: 1600 x 900mm (63 x 35½in). Other sizes made to client specification. www.fionazobole.co.uk

↑ **Flake** blind by Mia Cullin for Woodnotes. Made of Tyvek – fine, high-density polyethylene fibres. Individual elements can be combined for use as partitions or blinds. Supplied in packages of 160 pieces, which make an area of 2.5–4 sq m (27–43 sq ft). www.woodnotes.fi

← **Fabrics** tiles by Mirage Granito Ceramica. Porcelain stoneware tiles that replicate the appearance and texture of cloth. Available in six colours and two sizes: 600 x 600 or 1200 x 600mm (24 x 24 or 48 x 24in). www.mirage.it

→

Relax 737 by Aude Genton for Ruckstuhl. Limited-edition bed-cum-sofa-cum carpet. Wool felt made from 100 % pure virgin wool. Grey with metal buttons, varnished white. (W) 1800 x (L) 3000mm (71 x 118in). www.ruckstuhl.com

↑

MAJ by Mia Cullin for Alcro. Stencils in three shapes that can be combined in different configurations to create patterns on walls or other surfaces. www.alcro.se

→

ÄNG by Mia Cullin for Alcro. Wall stickers with 3D effect that can be painted in any colour. Polyester with adhesive back. www.alcro.se

↓

Hexagon lace carpet by
Kiki van Eijk. Handmade
using traditional
techniques. Wool.
(W) 1800 x (L) 2700mm
(71 x 106in). Different
sizes and colours available
on request.
www.kikiworld.nl

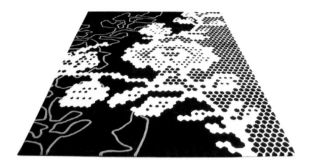

↑

IND-Industry by Inhabit.
Embossed wall flats
designed to expand
in any direction with
an automatic pattern
repeat. Can be used to
cover an existing wall,
disguise a rough surface,
or as decoration. Moulded
bamboo paper pulp
with off-white paintable
surface. Panels: 457 x
457mm (18 x 18in);
ten per box.
www.inhabitliving.com

←

SS-Seesaw by Inhabit.
Embossed wall flats
designed to expand
in any direction with
an automatic pattern
repeat. Can be used to
cover an existing wall,
disguise a rough surface
or as decoration. Moulded
bamboo paper pulp
with off-white paintable
surface. Panels: 457 x
457mm (18 x 18in);
ten per box.
www.inhabitliving.com

DOORS, WINDOWS AND STAIRS

→

James Soane

The architect James Soane is co-founder of Project Orange, a professional studio based in Clerkenwell, London. Since it was set up in 1997, the practice has won a reputation for attention to detail, manifested in its creative use of materials, colours and decoration to soften an otherwise modernist aesthetic. Recent projects include a £60 million fit-out of the new Radisson Cavan hotel in Co. Cavan, Ireland, and the Park Hotel in Mumbai, India. They are currently working on the first boutique hotel in Russia and an exclusive apartment building in London's Chelsea.

Soane is a great traveller, and wherever he goes in the world he directs his gaze upwards. 'Most of the time we concentrate on street level,' he says, 'which, although important, is only a fraction of the world around us. I always take a sketchbook with me, because the very act of putting pen to paper means you're looking again at something – no matter how poor the result. Last month I was in Cambodia, visiting the temples at Siem Reap, and was enchanted to discover a number of curious late modernist, French-style buildings commissioned by Prince Sihanouk in the 1960s. They were assured and elegant, built as official residences, and have now been turned into hotels, which is a brilliant example of how to preserve and revive old buildings.'

Project Orange's portfolio includes retail premises, hotels, schools, restaurants and new-builds – both apartments and one-off houses. In all their buildings, they give high priority to doors and windows – essential but often neglected details in any interior (or exterior) design scheme. 'Doors and windows are the most significant components in a building or room,' says Soane. 'The door is the physical threshold, while the window is the visual connection between one world and another – usually the inside and the outside. Doors signify how to enter and exit a room, while windows frame views and provide light. Both also give clues to the character of a place. It is not surprising that there are so many different designs for features whose function has been the same for hundreds of years. Modern technology makes it possible to have bigger bits of glass than before, so we are seeing larger windows and doors; the disadvantage of this is that large expanses of glass allow heat to escape from a building, even if there is double or triple glazing.'

In Soane's view, there are too many regulations affecting doors and windows in new buildings. 'The most important piece of information you need to know about a window is its thermal insulating capacity, or u-value. Any new building must have a high level of insulation so that heat isn't needlessly lost into the atmosphere. Windows tend to conduct heat to the outside, so you need to get the right balance between windows and wall. There must be no windows that children could fall out of – in the UK, this means that all windows must be a minimum height of 80cm (31½in) from the floor. Doors must be positioned in such a way that disabled people can operate them. Fire regulations also affect door construction. However, the actual design of a door should reflect the nature of the building or room and help people to orient themselves.'

Soane is dismissive about trends in interior design and architecture. 'I'm not sure I believe in trends any more as a useful concept,' he says. 'There are as many people ignoring new trends as following them. I see the design world more like a slightly dysfunctional community – everyone trying to exert influence over the next person. There is much copying, which can be alright. The real problem is that there is such a desire for quirky one-offs that the more fundamental question of how to create decent spaces for people to live in has been ignored. Of course, in Britain something like 90 per cent of buildings are not designed by architects. As time goes on, it will be increasingly important to hang on to what we've already got. Demolition is expensive and wasteful; our new buildings should be adaptable and constructed to last – none of which is very fashionable or sexy, but that's just too bad.'

Soane defines a good product as one that 'does what is says on the box', by which he means that it should be simple to install, to use and to understand. 'Anything with a gimmick should be discarded, and anything that says "fragile" when it shouldn't be fragile should be regarded with suspicion. Increasingly, we need to be asking ourselves: can it be fixed or maintained if it breaks or malfunctions? The problem with increasingly sophisticated technology is that, if you don't know how it works, you can't fix it.'

In a practice known for giving as much thought to the interior as to the exterior of buildings, details are key. 'How a door swings, a handle turns or a window tilts can transform it from being a mundane and inert component into something delightful and a work of art,' says Soane. 'The way buildings come together is evident in the detail of where one surface or finish meets another, or where one element is incorporated into the next. A detail may be complicated or simple – but it must be considered.'

Soane believes that scarcity of materials and resources will be a growing problem for architects and builders in the future. 'I specified a white marble last month,' he says. 'Last week I had a call to say that I couldn't have that marble. When I asked why not, the answer was as simple as it was chilling: "Because it has run out. There is no more." This is the future – except that it has already happened.'

←

ip-55 window series
by Antonio Citterio
for ipcompany (see
page 100).

→

Velux GDL Cabrio balcony window by Velux provides an instant balcony. As the lower section is moved forwards into position, integral banister railings are automatically raised to provide a sturdy and safe balcony surrounding. Toughened and laminated glass. Glazing option: Tempered/laminated/Argon/Krypton. (H) 2520 x (W) 942mm (99 x 37in). www.velux.com

↑

Celsius sliding glass system by Michael Glanz for DORMA. Depth of 56mm (2in) enables installation between two dry walls as well as in-wall and on-wall fixing. Low-energy operation. www.dorma.de

←

PERLA by Andrew Mauricedes for Erreti. Door handle from a set comprising door and window handle. Die-cast aluminium available with chrome, nickel or gold finishes. (L) 137 x (H) 67 x (D) 32mm (5½ x 2½ x 1in). www.erreti.com

←

Sliding door system by AVC. Single-structure door. Available in various finishes and glazing including glass, Plexiglas, plastic, aluminium or wood. Made to measure. www.avcnv.be

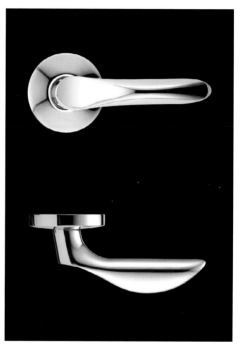

↑

FLOW by Eric Chan for Erreti. Door handle in die-cast aluminium with nickel, chrome or gold finishes. (L) 159.5 x (H) 70.5 x (D) 29.5mm (6 x 3 x 1in). www.erreti.com

←

Milano 400 by Dooria. Engineered timber doors, pre-finished in veneered and spray-painted – colours to client specification. Standard product: (H) 1940 or 2040 x (W) 625–925 x (D) 40mm (76 or 80 x 24½–36½ x 1½in). www.dooria.net

←

Pivoting doors (with or without floor spring) by AVC. Anodized aluminium frame with horizontal divisions. Materials: glass, Plexiglas, plastic, aluminium and timber. Lighting can also be inserted. Sliding version available. Made to measure.
www.avcnv.be

↑

Pavilion sliding door system by Antonio Citterio from the Classic collection for Tre Più. Any size available in natural wood finishes and coloured glass.
www.trep-trepiu.com

→

Acuity front door with sidelight by Kenneth Hepburn for Neoporte. Welded 16-gauge stainless steel and glass. Made to order. Dimensions up to: (H) 3048 x (W) 1372mm (120 x 54in).
www.neoporte.com

→

EMB403D stainless-steel doors by Forms + Surfaces. An affordable alternative to generic fire doors. Stainless steel with sandstone finish. Available in four distinctive configurations and a choice of metals, finishes and patterns. Standard sizes: (H) 1219–3048mm (51–120in). www.forms-surfaces.com

↓

Nieder 2 polyester folding door by Pierto Nieder for Tre Più. Space-saving design available in natural wood finishes and a wide range of lacquered colours. Various widths available, (H) 2150mm (84½in). www.trep-trepiu.com

←

Fullback double door by Kenneth Hepburn for Neoporte. Welded 16-gauge embossed stainless steel. Made to order. Double door dimensions: (H) 3048 x (W) up to 2743mm (120 x 108in). www.neoporte.com

Gira door handle by Jasper Morrison for Colombo. Available in polished brass, stainless steel, chrome or matt chrome. (W) 50 x (L) 143mm (2 x 5½in). www.colombodesign.it

→

ZH Duemilacinque H 356 door handle by Zaha Hadid and Woody Yao for Fusital Valli&Valli. Originally designed for Puerta America Hotel in Madrid. Nikrall zamak alloy, chrome and satin-finish chrome. (L) 150mm (6in). www.vallievalli.com

→

Meta handle by Konstantin Grcic for Colombo. Available in chrome or matt chrome. (W) 50 x (L) 143mm (2 x 5½in). www.colombodesign.it

←

EDO by Makio Hasuike for Colombo. Polished brass or matt chrome door lever. (W) 50 x (L) 137 x (D) 67mm (2 x 5½ x 2½in). www.colombodesign.it

←

Round doorknob by Colombo. Brass with gold, matt gold, chrome, matt chrome or bronze finishes. (W) 56 x (L) 109mm (2½ x 4½in). www.colombodesign.it

←

Zelda door handle by Jean Marie Massaud for Colombo. Available in bronze or matt chrome. (W) 52 x (L) 140mm (2 x 5½in). www.colombodesign.it

←

LUNA by Andrew Mauricides for Erreti. Die-cast aluminium in nickel, chrome or gold. (W) 68 x (L) 138 x (D) 40mm (3 x 5½ x 1½in). www.erreti.com

↓

FLUX05 by Mateli for Erreti. Comprises door and window set. Extruded aluminium in silver or black. (W) 60 x (L) 140 x (D) 26mm (2½ x 5½ x 1in). www.erreti.com

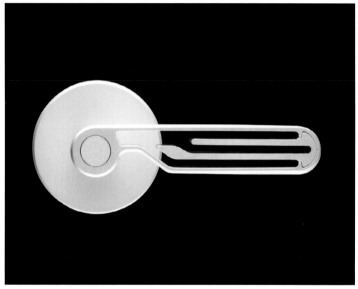

←

Logo by James Irvine for Olivari. Door handle in bio-chrome. (W) 52 x (L) 144mm (2 x 6in). www.olivari.it

↑

Rasomuro door by Lualdi
Porte. Glass or wood,
polished and matt-
lacquered, veneer. (H) to
2900 x (W) from 700mm
(114 x 27½in).
www.lualdiporte.com

↓

Synua by Oikos. Armoured
door comes with a wide
range of accessories
including door handles
and lighting. Various
finishes including wood,
lacquer or laminate.
Any size available.
www.oikos.it

←

Outline door by Gianni
Arnaudo and Erik Morvan
for Lualdi Porte. Wood,
polished and matt-
lacquered veneer.
www.lualdiporte.com

→

Quadra sliding door system by Massimo Luca for Albed. Aluminium with glass panelling available in a wide variety of glass and wood finishes. Made to measure.
www.albed.it

↑

Alpine range by Broxwood. High-efficiency window system. Made with two draught seals as standard, protection against heat loss, noise and weather. Available in white pine, larch or oak. Ultra low-maintenance. Aluminium-clad designs also available.
www.broxwood.com

←

Roto by Door 2000. Space-saving door is not hinged but rotates on a pivot and, therefore, opens in either direction. Available in four models and a wide variety of finishes including white enamel, blond walnut and dark cherry.
www.door-2000.com

→

Vista sliding door system by Massimo Luca for Albed. System designed to divide and furnish various rooms of the home or office. Doors guarantee flawless hermetic closure as they have functional seals to retain dust, and also ensure complete sound insulation. Various materials. Custom-made.
www.albed.it

→

SGG PRIVA-LITE by Saint-Gobain Glass. Liquid-crystal film sandwiched between sheets of laminated glass, permits glass to be transformed from clear to opaque at the click of switch. www.saint-gobain-glass.com

← **Valeria** by Giuseppe Bavuso for Rimadesio. Opening sliding panels with wenge frame and grey transparent glass. Other finishes available. Made to measure. www.rimadesio.it

→ **Recess Colour** grip door levers by Turnstyle Designs. Resin composite in coloured and metallic finishes. (W) 152 x (D) 60mm (6 x 2½in). www.turnstyledesign.com

↓ **Steel sliding window systems** designed by Schüco Jansen for Schüco International. Provide high level of thermal insulation, with appropriate fittings and glazing. Steel, various colours. Variable dimensions. www.schueco.com

↑ **OPALIKA** by SCHOTT. White-flashed opal glass – a colourless base glass with a thin white-flashed layer, ideal for light transmission. With minimum shadowing, has numerous architectural applications. Available in a variety of thicknesses from 2 to 6mm with dimensions of up to 1700 x 2400mm (67 x 94in). www.schott.com

←

Sliding glass door from the **Tuttovetro Collection – Tekna Line** by Henry glass. Triple sliding door in blue and orange lacquered glass, other colours available. Custom-made. www.henryglass.it

→

Schüco Window AWS ST. HI by Schüco International. Slimline steel high-insulation window system ideal for replacing old steel windows. Aluminium with polyester powder-coated colours or anodized finishes. Frame depth 70mm (3in). www.schueco.de

←

IMERA colour-effect glass by SCHOTT. Smooth, body-tinted glass suitable for interior and exterior applications. Available in a range of colours. Various thicknesses. www.schott.com

↓

E-slide electronic sliding door system by Schüco International. The e-drive system is integrated invisibly in the vent profile and includes anti-finger-trap software for complete safety in operation.

Suitable for vents weighing up to 250kg (555lb). Aluminium with polyester powder-coated colours or anodized finishes. Frame depth 120 and 160mm (5 and 6½in). www.schueco.com

↓

MIRONA from SCHOTT. Mineral glass coated on both sides with an optical layer to enable a defined degree of reflection and transparency. In front of a lit background, MIRONA looks like a transparent pane of glass; in front of a dark surface it acts as a mirror. www.schott.com

←

RIVULETTA by SCHOTT is a clear glass with a surface pattern of finely defined parallel lines on one side. Use for furniture, door glazing, room dividers, partition walls or shower cabinets. www.schott.com

→

LightPoints glass by SCHOTT allows LEDs to float freely inside glass and glow. Individual sized modules, flexible placement of LEDs and invisible wiring make it possible to cover any size area.
www.schott.com

← ↑

Narima colour-effect glass by SCHOTT. Dichroic glass producing dazzling colour and depth effects, depending on position, reflection and transmittance.
www.schott.com

→

Folding Façade SL 80 by Solarlux. Patented folding mechanism by which glazed panels are folded up and stacked away in a concertina action. Can be folded inwards or outwards. Aluminium, timber or timber/aluminium. Panel size up to 1000 x 3500mm (39 x 138in).
www.solarlux.com

→

Brighthandle Dot by Alexander Lervick for Brighthandle. Handle illuminates when room is busy – red for occupied, green for vacant. Other colour options available. Stainless steel. (L) 145 x (D) 20mm (6 x 1in). www.brighthandle.com

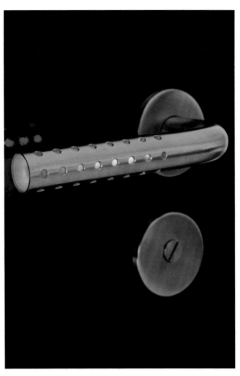

←

STADIP COLOR Glass by Saint-Gobain Glass. Laminated glass available in a wide range of transparent and translucent colours. www.saint-gobain-glass.com

SPD by SmartGlass International. Electronically switchable architectural glass that controls the amount of light, glare and heat passing through it. Reduces need for air conditioning in summer and heating in winter. Dark-blue glass in a variety of finishes including laser-etched and patterned. Bespoke, manufactured in a range of dimensions and thicknesses. www.smartglass international.com

Quadra Swing and sliding doors by Massimo Luca for Albed. Aluminium with glass panelling, available in a variety of finishes. Made to measure. www.albed.it

Folding Façade SL 35 for the modern balcony by Solarlux. When closed, an additional room is created; when opened, original balcony character is restored. Inwards or outwards opening direction. Aluminium, 35mm (1½in) thick. Standard glazing 5mm (¼in) float glass, but system capable of accepting sealed unit thicknesses up to 24mm (1in). Custom-made for any specification. www.solarlux.com

Sliding panels by Kvadrat and Silent Gliss. Choose between flat and folding panels in a wide range of fabrics. Can also be used as room divider. (W) 600 x maximum drop 3000m (23½ x 118in). www.silentgliss.co.uk

Slim pivoting frameless glass doors by Clear Divisions. Stainless steel with satin finish. Sliding fixed-glass doors also available. Made to measure. www.cleardivisions.co.uk

VF Cool window film by Vitrafol. When applied directly to glass, blocks 99 % of harmful ultraviolet light but rejects 55 % of total solar energy without noticeable reduction in light. Full-colour range or selection of graphic designs. www.vitrafol.com

←

Alu-wood fixed lights, window and balcony doors by Scandinavian Windows. Direct-glazed. Slim frame. Can be combined with opening lights in one frame. All shapes available. www.scandinavian-windows.co.uk

↓

TEMA range of internal sliding doors with one to four panels by ARC Systems. Aluminium and glass. Glass panels can be decorated to customer specification. Custom-made. www.arcs-ltd.co.uk

→

Pier by Studio Kairos for B&B Italia. Storage system with sliding doors that can close off both wall niches or form walk-in closets. Various finishes. www.bebitalia.it

→

Pirouette window shades by Hunter Douglas. Adjustable blinds with horizontal fabric vanes offer precise control of light. Available in forty-four textured-fabric combinations. (H) 381–3048 x (W) 305–3658mm (15–120 x 12–144in). www.hunterdouglas.com

↑

Bespoke glass design by Apropos. Glass structures to complement the character and style of your home. All structures finished using polyester powder-coated aluminium, available in a wide colour range and Pilkington K glass. www.apropos-conservatories.com

→

STADIP COLOR glass partition by Saint-Gobain Glass. Range of coloured laminated glass. Using any combination of a range of colour films, virtually any colour, translucent or transparent glass, can be created. Made to measure. www.saint-gobain-glass.com

←

SECURIT toughened safety glass by Saint-Gobain Glass. Heat-treated to increase strength and resistance to impact. Approximately five times more resistant than normal glass. www.saint-gobain-glass.com

→

Pilkington Activ Neutral Glass. Self-cleaning solar-control glass, ideal for hard-to-clean areas. Solar-control coating also helps keep internal temperatures cooler. Neutral-coloured glass. Custom-made. www.pilkingtonselfcleaningglass.co.uk

↓

Frame system for Atlante storage and wall system by Studio Kairos for B&B Italia. Includes chest of drawers and clothes rail. www.bebitalia.it

↓
FXi windows by Cantifix. Range includes tilt and turn, pivot, top/side-hung. Butt hinges or friction stays. Minimum size (top-hung) from 400 x 400mm (16 x 16in). Maximum size (tilt and turn) 1300 x 2100 or 1600 x 1800mm (51 x 83 or 63 x 71in). www.cantifix.co.uk

↑
Heavy-duty sliding doors by Cantifix. 63mm- (2½in-) deep tracks can be coupled together to accommodate a number of sliding or fixed leafs. www.cantifix.co.uk

↑
FXi casement door by Cantifix. Can be single or double opening. Powder-coated aluminium frame available in wide range of colours and sizes. www.cantifix.co.uk

→

CD sliding doors by Cantifix. Heavy-duty design. Siding leafs can be used in conjunction with structurally glazed fixed panels to give minimal appearance. Powder-coated aluminum and glass. (H) up to 3000mm (118in). www.cantifix.co.uk

↓

MC curtain walling by Cantifix. Clean and narrow sight lines. Façades can be faceted to create more interesting shapes and sizes. www.cantifix.co.uk

↑

Bonded silicone-jointed **glass roof lights** by Cantifix. Glass is able to span up to 1700mm (67in) without deflecting. www.cantifix.co.uk

PLANITHERM glass by Saint-Gobain Glass. Transparent metallic-coated glass reflects heat from radiators or fires back into the room, rather than allowing it to escape through windows. At the same time it allows free heat and light from the sun to pass through the glass, warming the interior and further contributing to energy efficiency of the windows. www.saint-gobain-glass.com

↑
GXi sliding doors by Cantifix. Single, double or triple track to accommodate any number of sliding or fixed leafs. Powder-coated aluminium and glass. Door heights up to 3000mm (118in). www.cantifix.co.uk

←
SFK70 folding doors by Sunfold. Panels up to 3000mm (118in) high can be hinged together in long 'trains' to open up 90 % of an elevation. Maximum panel width is 1000mm (39in) for heights up to 2300mm (90½in). Aluminium frames coloured to suit taste. www.sunfold.com

→

Diamant by Saint-Gobain Glass. Extra-clear glass with optical qualities. The low iron content in this glass produces a higher light transmittance and a reduced green tint inherent of other glasses. www.saint-gobain-glass.com

↓

Bioclean self-cleaning glass by Saint-Gobain Glass. Dual-action glass that stays cleaner for longer. A permanent, transparent coating on the outside surface of the glass harnesses the power of sun and rain to break down and remove dirt and grime. www.selfcleanglass.com

↑

Sliding door by Schwering. Part of the Fine Art range. Stainless-steel running rail fixtures. Finishes in zebrano, maple, oak, Anegre, wenge or white-painted. Made to measure. www.schwering.de

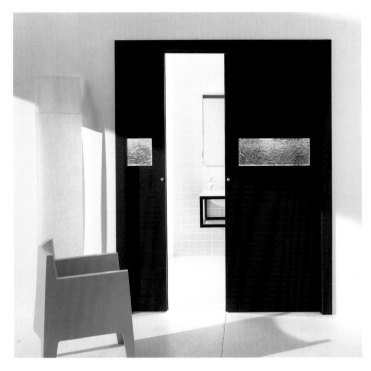

↑

Barraocean from the
Avant system by Francesco
Policci for Domina.
Handmade door panel
with glass mosaic inset.
Available in wenge, pear,
sessile oak or maple, and
in a wide range of colours
and finishes.
www.dominaporte.it

↓

Line One letterbox by
Atelier 522 for Serafini.
Stainless and black
powder-coated steel.
Has separate matching
newspaper slot. (H) 360 x
(W) 360 x (D) 100mm
(14 x 14 x 4in).
www.serafini.de

←

Concrete letterbox by
Atelier 522 for Serafini.
Front and side casing
made of 15mm- (½in-)-
thick concrete. Available
in grey or sandstone with
stainless-steel shutter.
(H) 474 x (W) 320 x
(D) 113mm
(18½ x 12½ x 4½in).
www.serafini.de

←

Square letterbox by Atelier 522 for Serafini. Powder-coated steel available in nine colours. (H) 360 x (W) 360 x (D) 100mm (14 x 14 x 4in). www.serafini.de

↓

Luminette privacy sheers by Hunter Douglas. Translucent fabric facings and soft fabric vanes that rotate for infinite degrees of light control and privacy. Any colour desired. (H) 610–3048 x (W) 305–4877mm (24in–120 x 12–192in). www.hunterdouglas.com

→

XL 04 by Gruppo AIP, from the Trix collection. Smooth panelled wood door with aluminium inserts, shown here in Rovere wenge. Also available in cherry, walnut and oak. (H) 2400 x (W) 2100 x (D) 800mm (94 x 83 x 31½in). www.aipporte.com

←

Wall and door by Lualdi Porte. Wood-panelling system, which creates or conceals niches for wardrobes, bookcases, cupboards and so on. www.lualdiporte.com

↑

Metal Stile and Rail doors by Forms+Surfaces. Sandstone finish, stainless steel and Epsilon pattern glass. System elements can be specified in limitless combinations of materials, finishes and three-dimensional patterns to create custom-looking doors. Standard sizes: (H) 2134 x (W) 914mm or (H) 2438 x (W) 914mm (84 x 36 or 96 x 36in). www.forms-surfaces.com

→

Letterman 11 mailbox by Michael Rösing for Radius Design. Stainless steel in a range of six colours. (H) 340 x (W) 400 x (D) 115mm (13½ x 16 x 4½in). www.radius-design.com

Flush letterbox by SSS Siedle. Door loudspeaker with light module. Polished steel in wide range of colours. Approx (H) 600 x (W)150mm (23½ x 6in). www.siedleusa.com

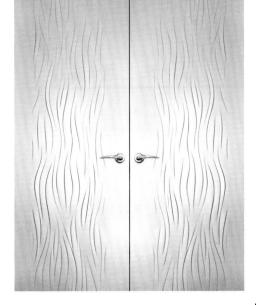

↑

EMB402D architectural metal door by Forms+ Surfaces. Embossed doors available in four distinctive configurations and a variety of metals, finishes, patterns and colour. An alternative to generic fire doors. Standard sizes: (H) 2134 x (W) 914mm or (H) 2438 x (W) 914mm. (84 x 36 or 96 x 36in). Other sizes available on request. www.forms-surfaces.com

↓

Diana by Studio Olivari. Door handle. Brass, available in three finishes. (H) 197 x (W) 35 x (D) 52 mm (8 x 1½ x 2in). www.olivari.it

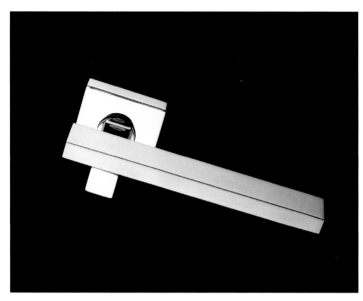

← Time-Space 'Q' by Alessandro Mendini for Olivari. Handle available for doors, windows and double-hung windows. Brass with various finishes. (W) 58 x (L) 153mm (2½ x 6in). www.olivari.it

↓ Infinity by Giorgio and Max Pajetta for Olivari. Handle available for doors, with rosette or plate as well as for windows and double-hung windows. Polished or matt chrome with crystal in a wide range of colours. (H) 27 x (L) 153 x (D) 71mm (1 x 6 x 3in). www.olivari.it

← ECO207D with 1200 Eco-Etch door from the Architectural Metal series by Forms+Surfaces. Steel with satin finish. Different materials and finishes available. Standard sizes: (H) 2134 x (W) 914mm or (H) 2438 x (W) 914mm (84 x 36 or 96 x 36in). Other sizes available on request. www.forms-surfaces.com

→
Sky-Frame frameless insulated sliding windows by Skyframe. System for large-surface sliding windows whose surrounding frame can be installed flush with walls, ceilings and floors, allowing unrestricted views. Dimensions to client specification. www.skyframe.ch

→
Venere lever by Alessandro Mendini for Olivari. Available for doors with rosette or plate, and windows and double-hung windows. Polished or matt chrome with crystal in a wide range of colours. (H) 30 x (L) 141 x (D) 60mm (1 x 5½ x 2½in). www.olivari.it

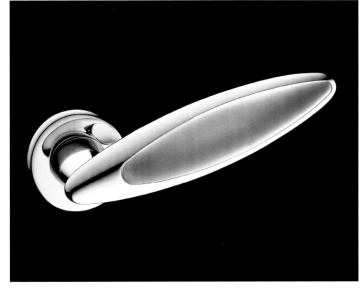

←
Door station with integrated letterbox by Renz Gira. Can be integrated in a variety of letterbox units for flush-mounted, surface-mounted or free-standing installation. Available for order with cut-outs for call buttons, door speakers and so on. www.gira.com

Lever handle model 1194
by Hartmut Weise for FSB.
Satin-finished stainless
steel or mirror-polish finish.
(L) 134 x (D) 64mm
(5 x 2½in).
www.fsb.de

←

**H 350 Serie CA
Duemiladue** designed
by Cerri&Associati. Door
lever in polished or satin
chrome. Custom finishes
available. (W) 65 x (L) 150
x (D) 53mm (2½ x 6 x 2in).
www.vallivalli-us.com

←

Tacta door lever by
Carlo Bartoli for Colombo
Design. Brass in various
colour finishes. (W) 48 x
(L) 126mm (2 x 5in).
www.colombodesign.it

←

H315 Serie G Novanta by
Pierluigi Cerr for Valli&Valli.
Spring-assisted door
lever with built-in rosette.
Polished brass, white
enamel, polished chrome.
Custom finishes also
available. (W) 65 x
(L) 109 x (D) 48mm
(2½ x 4 x 2in).
www.vallivalli-us.com

←

H343 Serie JP Duemilla
by John Pawson for
Valli&Valli. Door lever in
polished or satin chrome.
Custom finishes available.
(W) 65 x (L) 150 x
(D) 53mm (2½ x 6 x 2in).
www.vallivalli-us.com

←

Lever handle 185 by
Hewi. Stainless steel with
textured finishes.
(L) 134 x (D) 64mm
(5 x 2½in).
www.hewi.co.uk

←

FSB lever handles 1063
by Christophe Ingenhoven
for FSB. Aluminium,
AluGrey, stainless steel.
Grip applications, wenge
and oak, dark grey plastic
or white, red and black
Corian. (L) 135 x
(D) 60mm (5½ x 2½in).
www.fsb.de

←

**H351 Serie AR
Duemiladue** by Alan
Ritchie-Philip of Johnson
Architects for Valli&Valli.
Door lever, polished
chrome or satin chrome.
(W) 65 x (L) 133 x
(D) 58mm (2½ x 5 x 2in).
www.vallivalli-us.com

←

Walchwindow04
window and façade
system by Andreas Moll
for Walchfenster. System
with opening glass panes.
Optional fitting allows
windows to be reversed
by 165 degrees, making
it possible to clean both
sides of windowpanes
from the inside.
www.walchfenster.at

↑
OPTION 5 by Urban Front.
Stainless-steel door handle
with backplate in chrome
finish. (H) 200 x
(W) 200mm (8 x 8in).
www.urbanfront.co.uk

→
ip-55 window series
by Antonio Citterio for
ipcompany. Collection of
windows for house fronts.
Narrow frames means
windows allow approx
10 % more daylight into
the room while providing
high thermal insulation
levels. Suitable for almost
any façade. Wood or
aluminium frames.
Various dimensions.
www.ipcompany.de

Sorrento V by Nabil Assaf
for Urban Front. Front
door with flush vision
panel designed. Natural
oak, stainless-steel panel,
security glass. (H) 2400 x
(W) 1050mm (94 x 41in).
www.urbanfront.co.uk

↓

Rondo by Elizabeth
Assaf for Urban Front.
Dark-brown wenge with
stainless steel. (H) 2100 x
(W) 2000mm (83 x 79in).
www.urbanfront.co.uk

↑

Ferrara front door by Nabil
Assaf for Urban Front.
Reinforced steel, solid
American walnut.
(H) 2100 x (W) 1050mm
(83 x 41in).
www.urbanfront.co.uk

← **Porto** glass entrance door by Nabil Assaf for Urban Front. Shown in iroko-stained ebony, with two side lights in sandblasted glass with etched numerals. (H) 2300 x (W) 1700mm (90½ x 67in). www.urbanfront.co.uk

↓ **Cobbles** by Bill McColl for Sculptural Glass Doors. Wood with mahogany veneer and ClearCast glass. Available in a selection of glass tints. (H) 2032 x (W) 914mm (80 x 36in). www.sculpturalglass doors.com

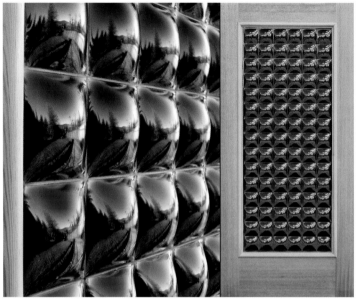

← **Sliding French window** in aluminium and wood by Buonanno. Ideal for wide spaces with panoramic views. Bespoke design available in a variety of wood and aluminium finishes. www.buonannospa.com

↑ ←

Bloomframe window balcony by Hofman Du Jardin Architects. Window frame can be transformed into a balcony with one simple movement. Size, material and colour of balcony to client specification.
www.bloomframe.nl
www.hurks.nl

←

Universe sliding door
by Dooria. Space-saving
design makes it possible
to mount a sliding door
externally on a wall.
Oak with 10mm (½in)
tempered glass. Available
in six types of glass
including clear, antique
or smoked. (H) 1940 or
2040mm x (W) 625, 725,
825 or 925mm (76 or 80 x
24½, 28½, 32½ or 36½in).
Some models can be
custom-made.
www.dooria.net

↓

D01 sliding door system
by Torben Mogensen
for Mogdesign. Frame
in anodized aluminium,
panels available in
melamine, mirror, painted
glass, veneer or Perspex
finishes. Available in white,
black and a range of
colours. Made to measure.
www.mogdesignonline.co.uk

←

Keyhole door detail
by Philip Watts. Cast
aluminium, Georgian wired
glass, sand-blasted logos
and bright polish finishes
also available. (W) 290 x
(L) 580mm (11½ x 23in).
www.philipwatts
design.com

←

**DW127 FSB 1723
LED roses** by FSB.
Illuminated keyhole emits
soft light for interior or
exterior use. Aluminium,
AluGrey, stainless steel,
bronze or brass with
various coloured lights.
(Diameter) 55mm (2in).
www.fsb.de

↑

Modular wall system by
AVC. Modular elements
with thin separation
strip, easy and quick to
assemble with AVC clip
system. Various materials
including glass, Plexiglas,
synthetic materials and
timber. Thickness 47 or
150mm (2 or 6in).
www.avcnv.be

→

Oslo front door by Elizabeth Assaf for Urban Front. Shown here in European oak; stained light oak with two side-lights in sand-blasted glass. Overall dimensions: (H) 2100 x (W) 1600mm (83 x 63in). Door size: (H) 2000 x (W) 950mm (79 x 37½in). www.urbanfront.co.uk

→

Addera by Dooria. Engineered timber, pre-finished in wenge-stained oak with walnut panel. Also available in a wide range of finishes and colours. (H) 1940 or 2040 x (W) 625, 725, 825 or 925mm (76 or 80 x 24½, 28½, 32½ or 36½in). Some models can be custom-made. www.dooria.net

←

Merit 30E1 door by Dooria. Engineered timber, pre-finished with clear glass, veneered and spray-painted to colour of client's choice. (H) 1940 or 2040 x (W) 625, 725, 825 or 925mm (76 or 80 x 24½, 28½, 32½ or 36½in). Some models can be custom-made. www.dooria.net

→

Amoeba by Philip Watts of Philip Watts Design. Circular pulls. Cast aluminium. (W) 243 x (L) 276 x (D) 80mm (9½ x 11 x 3in). www.philipwatts design.com

→

3010 Exclusiv Line

front door by Wermer Kemming for Keratuer. Multifunctional stainless-steel bar handle houses a doorbell/intercom unit and a fingerprint module for individual access authorization. The personal fingerprint and/or the portable wireless transmitter replaces the key and serves as opening signal for the KeraMatic safety interlock. Door height up to 2800mm (110in). www.keratuer.de

←

Sliding door system

by Eclisse. Supplied as complete unit including door in a variety of wood veneers. Available in many different sizes. www.eclisse.co.uk

Sequoia by Kenneth Hepburn for Neoporte. Welded 16-gauge 100 % stainless steel and glass door complete with fully integrated system. Dimensions (H) 3048 x (W) 1420mm (120 x 56in) for a total double opening of (H) 3048 x (W) 2743mm (129 x 108in). www.neoporte.com

← **C-Wand** sliding door by Adrian Welter for Welterwall. Sliding door requiring no lintel or hinge, while gliding mechanism is concealed within the door itself. Consists of two slabs that can be made in materials including glass, plastic and wood. Each slab can be separately designed and executed in a different material. Height is user-defined. www.welterwall.de

← **Milano 481** door by Dooria. Pre-finished engineered timber, veneered and spray-painted to colour of client's choice. Standard product: (H) 1940 or 2040mm x (W) 625–925mm (76 or 80 x 24½–36½in). Some models can be custom-made. www.dooria.net

→ **Mistral** by Siller Treppen from the Innovation series. Straight quarter or half-turned staircase, custom-made in glass. Stainless steel and various woods. www.sillertreppen.com

← **3010.1** front door by Julian Kemming for Keratuer. Multifunctional stainless-steel door handle conceals a special profile cylinder lock behind a rotatable front panel for conventional closing, as well as a fingerprint module for individual access authorization. Glass, wood, stainless steel. Door height up to 2800mm (110in) www.keratuer.de

→ **SkidMark** tyre track door pull by Philip Watts of Philip Watts Design. Can be used in 1–2m (3–6ft) lengths. Dual-function, can also used as a kickplate across bottom of door. Cast aluminium. (W) 120 x (L) 1000mm (5 x 39in). www.philipwatts design.com

← **Europa** glass staircase by Siller Treppen. Custom-made straight quarter or half-turned staircase. Shown here in glass and stainless steel; other materials available. www.sillertreppen.com

↓ **Block** staircase by Limestone Gallery. Bespoke floating staircase manufactured in solid blocks of white Limeira limestone. www.limestonegallery.com

↑ **SWING** suspended wood staircase by Cast. Lamellar beech step with stainless-steel edge guard. Staircase width 600–1000mm (23½–39in). www.castscale.it

→

Knock metal-frame staircase with wooden steps by Rintal Spa. Modular stairs with central structure and adjustable tread. Various wood and metal finishes, oven-painted with epoxy powders or glossy galvanic chromium plating. www.rintal.com

→

Attik Fly Stairs by Scala. Metal/timber/stainless steel/glass frame staircase. www.scalainteriors.com

→

Nika modular staircase by Mobirolo. Aluminium, timber and stainless-steel modular staircase available in various shapes and unlimited range of timber and colours. Made to measure. www.mobirolo.com

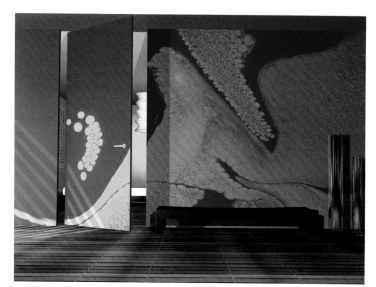

↓ →

L'Invisibile bookcase door (turns through 360 degrees) by Portarredo Design for Erreti. Available in any shape, size or form. Panels are available in any material. Custom-made. www.linvisibile.it

→

SEGMENTA by Mauro Lipparini for Misuraemme. Wardrobe with sliding doors, bronzed mirrors with inserts in oak brown. (H) 2582 x (W) 4372 x (D) 650mm (102 x 172 x 25½in). www.misuraemme.it

←

Sliding glass door from the Tuttovetro Collection – Tekna Line by Henry glass. Red-lacquered glass with Isy frame in aluminium. Available in a wide range of colours. Custom-made. www.henryglass.it

RS [R]EVLUTION

←
Automatic Disappearing
sliding door by Portarredo Design for Erreti. Custom-made. Maximum height 3000 x (W) 1200mm (118 x 47in).
www.linvisibile.it

←
Vento Therm by Schüco International. Insulated PVC-U window system with continuous air exchange, pollen filter, heat recovery and solar installation. Custom-made to fit.
www.schueco.com

↑
Range 120 Lever Handle designed by Delugan Meissl Associated Architects for Hewi. Synthetic material with steel core in the join area. High-gloss or black matt.
www.hewi.com

↑ →
E façade by Schüco
International. Harnesses
solar thermal energy using
large-scale units with
integrated translucent
flat-plate collectors. Louvre
blades provide lightly
patterned transparency.
Custom-made to fit.
www.schueco.com

Chapter three

HEATING AND COOLING

→

Paul Priestman

Paul Priestman is one of the founders of Priestman Goode, an award-winning design consultancy whose many and diverse projects include BT Home Hub communications equipment and Yotel compact hotel rooms, as well as aeroplane interiors. One of the firm's most successful products is an iconic heating radiator: a simple, vertical, stainless-steel coil manufactured by Bisque and made in Italy – indeed, 'Hot Spring' is Bisque's bestselling radiator worldwide. 'I designed Hot Spring in 1996,' says Priestman. 'There have been plenty of designer radiators on the market in recent years, but what's exceptional about this one is that it's been so amazingly successful.' Hot Spring has won awards in many countries, including China. Priestman attributes its success to a number of factors, but perhaps the most important is that it was one of the first radiators to be designed as an upright rather than a horizontal installation. 'Why use up useful space?' was the question that inspired this innovation.

'The thinking for Hot Spring came from a method of manufacture,' explains Priestman. 'Radiators are complicated to make. There's a great deal of cutting and welding, which uses lots of energy and material. Hot Spring is made from one continuous length of tube, which is formed into a spiral shape by a special computer-controlled machine. It's quicker and easier to make than other radiators and it has fewer joins, so it's very heat-efficient. Radiators need a large surface area because their job is to transfer the hot-water temperature into air. If you were able to look inside industrial machines, you would see that they use coils, because the coil is a very efficient means of heat exchange.'

Another reason for the success of Hot Spring is that it represents a pleasing marriage between the highly functional and the perfectly formed. So was it function or form that took priority in the design? 'For me,' says Priestman, 'design is all to do with making something better. Of course, it has to be beautiful – that's a given. Design is really good when there is nothing superfluous. If you can't take anything away and you can't add anything, it means that the object is less fashion-orientated, which is very important in radiators. You want a classic design, something pleasing – not something that's going to jump out at you, but something that works. A lot of decorative radiators are highly inefficient.' The design of Hot Spring is constantly evolving – for example, the company has just launched a mini version. 'There's something about a spiral that makes people just want to go up to and touch,' says Priestman. 'We did a version with thermochromatic paint so when it was cold it was black and when it was warm it was red. The great thing about it was that you could see when your radiator was on rather than having

to feel it. There are plenty of technologies like that coming through.'

Heating is one of the least explored aspects of product design for interiors, but Priestman's involvement in this area dates from his days as a student at the Royal College of Art, where he designed a set of radiators. 'I noticed that a great deal of effort was being put into lighting design and that sort of thing,' he says. 'By comparison, a radiator was no more than a piece of pressed metal on the wall. I started to wonder why heating couldn't be made more interesting.'

Radiator design, in general, is the area that attracts least interest or enquiry in terms of design, either in the domestic or the commercial environment. So why is it still the case that the average radiator is no more than 'a piece of pressed metal on the wall'? In Priestman's view, there are areas of product design that are stuck in a backwater. 'In some cases, a manufacturing process has been set up somewhere – in China, say – that has made it so cheap to produce a particular item that it's very difficult for other people to invest in that product area because they will be undercut. Desk fans, for instance – you won't find any of the big brands going into desk fans because you can buy one for five quid around the corner. You can go to a DIY store and buy a radiator off the shelf for nine or ten pounds.' Priestman Goode are currently working on a project to try to compete with these mass-market producers – a design for a flatbed radiator that conceals the heat exchanger at the back.

Our heating expectations have changed much in recent years. 'Under-floor heating is becoming more common in new-builds because it is quite efficient and makes spaces more flexible,' says Priestman. 'However, in the case of houses that already have condensing and combination boilers, which are so efficient, I think radiators are here to stay. Flexible manufacturing has also helped, and there are now new manufacturers coming into the market and more choice of radiators.

Priestman's advice to anyone installing radiators is to invest in the ones that will be on show rather than those hidden behind furniture. 'Splash out on one or two elements, maybe in the bathroom and kitchen,' he says, but he believes there is no need to install expensive radiators throughout the house. 'The other thing that's happening in the housing market,' Priestman points out, 'is that homes are much better insulated than they used to be, so you need fewer heating products. Also, in the past, if you decided to update the heating in your home, you'd call in a plumber to install the lot. You might choose where the radiator should go, but you wouldn't choose the radiator itself. Now you choose the fittings.'

←

Saturn and Moon Radiator by Peter Rankin for Antrax (see page 150).

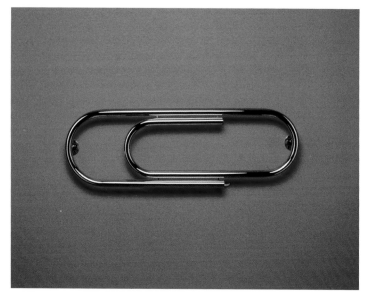

←

Towelclip by Eskimo. Compact, low-energy electric towel rail in range of colours. (H) 250 x (W) 815 x (D) 85mm (10 x 32 x 3½in). www.eskimodesign.co.uk

→

Varde Line 22 by Varde Ovne. Updated version of wood-burning stove in grey steel. (H) 260 or 380 x (W) 300 x (D) 280mm (10½ or 15 x 12 x 11in). www.vardeovne.dk

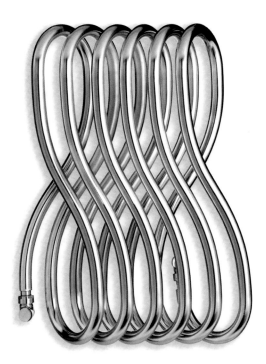

←

Arabesque by Ron Arad
for Tubor. Hot-water
radiator. Inox steel electro-
polished. (H) 580 x
(L) 500mm (23 x 20in).
www.ripples.ltd.uk

↓
Balance Mobile by
Peter Maly for Conmoto.
Open, smoke-free, flueless
fireplace fuelled by liquid
bio-alcohol. Also available
as stand-alone version with
stainless-steel base for
floor- or wall-mounting.
Fire chamber: (H) 600 x
(W) 900 x (D) 500mm
(24 x 35½ x 20in).
www.conmoto.com

←

Heatwave electric radiator by Joris Laarman for Droog Design. Aluminium and polyurethane. (H) 2100 x (W) 950 x (D) 50mm (83 x 37½ x 2in). www.droogdesign.nl

↓

Wishknot by Tubor. Aluminium hot-water radiator with 17 Swarovski crystals. (H) 200 x (W) 200 x (D) 55mm (23½ x 23½ x 2in). www.ripples.ltd.uk

↑

Anthracite by Planika. Bio fireplace in steel and tempered glass. Burns environmentally friendly Fanola fuel. (H) 820 x (W) 1100 x (D) 436mm (32½ x 43½ x 17½in). www.planikadecor.com

→

Zana-Plinth by Frederik Aerts for Thermic Designer Radiators. Hot-water radiator comprised of horizontal steel tubes and two integrated steel collectors of 3mm welded steel plate. Available in over 100 colours. (H) 254 x (W) 1000–3000mm (10 x 39½–118in). www.thermic.be

←

Loungefire by Carsten Gollnick for Conmoto. Wall-mounted fire fuelled with bio-alcohol. Gloss black or white finish. Burning chamber in brushed stainless steel. Additional modular units available. Basic element with fireplace (H) 300 x (W) 1000 x (D) 400mm (12 x 39½ x 16in). www.conmoto.com

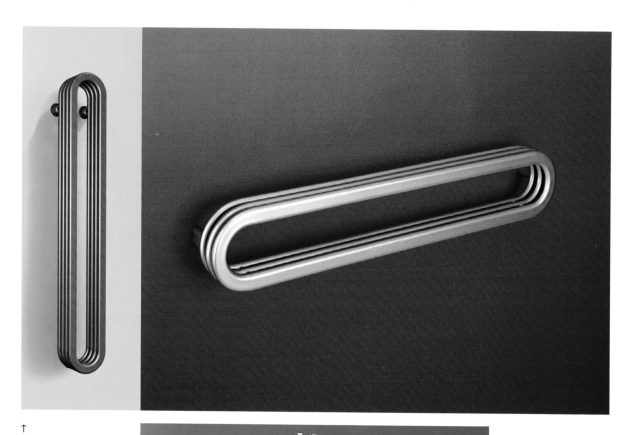

↑

Outline by Paul Priestman for Bisque. Hot-water radiator in coiled steel tubing. Can be mounted horizontally or vertically. Available in white, aluminium or acid green. Available in three sizes. Vertical: (H) 1200, 1500 or 1800mm (47½, 59 or 71in). Horizontal: (W) 1000, 1400 or 1800mm (39½, 55 or 71in).
www.bisque.co.uk

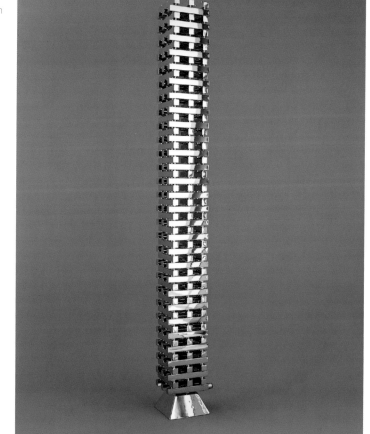

←

Zanzibar by Francesco Dori of TalinDori for Bisque. Hot-water radiator in chrome or Argenta textured metallic finish. (H) 1250 or 1790mm (49½ or 70½in).
www.bisque.co.uk

←

Chromifocus by Dominique Imbert of Focus. Wood-burning or gas-fuelled fire. Colours as shown. (H) 1000 x (W) 1000mm (39½ x 39½in). www.focus-creation.com

↓

Hot Hoop by Paul Priestman for Bisque. Hot-water radiator in coiled tubing finished in high-shine, mirror, matt, lustre, aluminium, lilac and white. Three sizes. (Diameter) 500, 700 and 900mm (20, 28 and 35½in). www.bisque.co.uk

←

Domino by Matteo Thun for Tubor. Sectional, flexible hot-water radiator. Die-cast aluminium, glossy or satin finish in various colours. Each Domino section measures (H) 200 x (W) 200mm (8 x 8in).
www.ripples.ltd.uk

→

Parrett by Myson. Hot-water radiator. Stainless-steel cylindrical tower features internal coil, giving maximum heat output while taking up minimal space. (H) 1810 x (W) 190mm (71½ x 7½in).
www.myson.co.uk

←

Domino by Britta von Tasch for Cera Design. Compact wood-burning fire with soot-free furnace. Available in silver, iron-grey or matt-black varnish. (H) 1005 x (W) 435mm (39½ x 17in).
www.cera.de

↓

Planet by Tubes Radiators. Flat-tube hot-water radiator, part of the Basics collection. Steel construction available as a single or double radiator in both vertical and horizontal versions in a wide range of sizes. Vertical: (H) 1200–3000 x (W) 210–980mm (47½–118 x 8½–39in). Horizontal: (H) 210–980 x (W) 50–4600mm (8½–39 x 2–181in). www.tubesradiatori.com

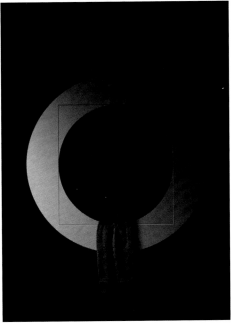

↑
La Quadraturadelcerchio by Ridea. Aluminium hot-water radiator, available in a variety of colours and finishes. (Diameter) 600 or 800mm (24 or 31½in). www.ridea.it

→

Balance by Peter Maly for Conmoto. Modular wood-burning stove system. Storage elements and bench can be combined in a variety of ways. Grey powder-coated steel finish. Also available in oak and walnut and as a compact version. Fire chamber: (H) 600 x (W) 900mm (24 x 35½in). Side elements: (W) 600, 900 or 1200mm (24, 35½ or 47½in). Bench: (W) 1200mm (47½in). www.conmoto.com

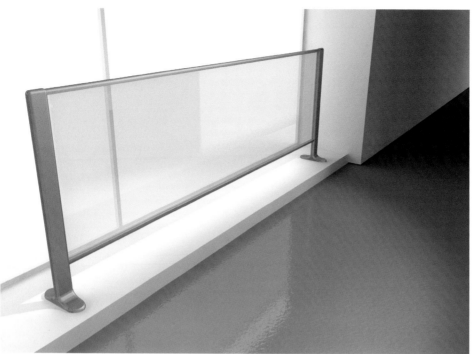

←

Glassy by Gruppo Ragaini. Electric radiator available in different colours with customized surface detail. Can also be supplied with mirror layers.
(H) 400–600mm x
(L) 1200 (16–24 x 47½in).
www.grupporagaini.com

↓

ONE by No Picnic for Tubor. Electric or hot-water radiator. Incorporates mirror, digital clock and calendar. Steel construction. Available in two sizes: (H) 520–1440 x (W) 94–520mm (20½–57 x 4–20½in).
www.ripples.ltd.uk

↑

Firebelly FB by James Clegg for Firebelly Woodstoves. Wood-burning stove available in wide choice of colours including charcoal and pewter. (H) 530 x (W) 411 x (D) 326mm (21 x 16 x 13in).
www.firebellyshop.com

→

Igloo by EcoSmart. Rectangular free-standing fire designed to accept the EcoSmart flueless burner. Comprising toughened-glass frame, back and sides and non-combustible floating stainless-steel shelf. (H) 900 x (W) 977 x (D) 490mm (35½ x 39 x 19½in). www.ecosmartfire.com

↑ →

Mod.U by Federico Gaudino for Gruppo Ragaini. Aluminium hot-water radiator in white. Each mosaic square is a heating plate. (H) 800 x (W) 800mm (31½ x 31½in). www.grupporagaini.com

→

Modern Grate by
EcoSmart. Low-line
rectangular grate with
built-in EcoSmart burner in
stainless steel. Rust-treated
steel, finished in matt
black with Teflon coating.
(H) 167 x (W) 550 x (D)
448mm (7 x 22 x 18in).
www.ecosmartfire.com

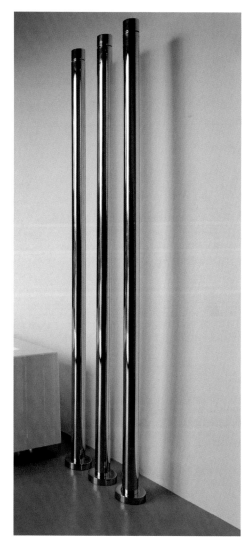

← ↑

TBT by Ludovica and
Roberto Palomba for
Tubes. Chromed brass
tube, also available in
black or white. Can be
mounted horizontally
or vertically. Available
as hydraulic, electric or
dual-function version.
(L) 1200–2000 x
(Diameter) 70mm
(47½–79 x 3in).
www.tubesradiatori.com

←

Tubone radiator by Andrea Crosetta for Antrax. 60mm (2½in) continuous steel tubing, available in twenty-two colours and fourteen special finishes. Can be mounted horizontally or vertically. Single radiator (illustrated): (H) 1500 x (W) 210mm (59 x 8½in). Double and triple versions also available.
www.antrax.it

↓

Fire Box by Planika. Flueless, stainless-steel unit using environmentally friendly Fanola fuel. (H) 100 x (W) 400 x (D) 280mm (4 x 6 x 11in).
www.planikadecor.com

↓

Travelmate by Studio Vertijet for Conmoto. Mobile fireplace. Flueless design for indoor/outdoor use. Black powder-coated stainless steel. (H) 500 x (W) 700 x (D) 200mm (20 x 28 x 8in).
www.conmoto.com

→

Skin by James di Marco for Caleido. Hot-water radiator, double version also available. Steel, available in a wide range of colours. (H) 2040 x (W) 503 x (D) 125mm. www.caleido.bs.it

↑

Honey, by James di Marco for Caleido. Hot-water radiator, steel, available in a wide range of colours. (H) 2200 x (W) 650 x (D) 125mm (86½ x 25½ x 5in). www.caleido.bs.it

←

Dancing Flames 200 by Kal-Fire. Open gas fire, uses natural or propane gas. (H) 2000 x (W) 4050 x (D) 1955mm (79 x 159½ x 77in). www.kal-fire.nl

→

Miofocus by Dominique Imbert of Focus. Compact, wall-mounted fireplace, wood- or gas-fuelled. Steel wall 2.5mm thick. Available in heat-resistant matt-black or anthracite-grey paint. (H) 600 x (L) 950 x (D) 500mm (24 x 37½ x 20in). www.focus-creation.com

↓

Firemaster 515 by Esse. Flueless log-effect gas stove with catalytic converter. Steel construction with black or grey finish. (H) 596 x (W) 430 x (D) 267mm (24 x 17 x 10½in). www.esse.com

↑

Diablo by Drugasar. Hanging gas fire, part of the DRU Designer collection. Balanced fuel or LPG. Available in four finishes: alu-metallic, sand-metallic, anthracite and stainless steel. (H) 685 x (W) 560 x (D) 375mm (27 x 22 x 15in). www.drugasar.co.uk

Renzofocus by Dominique
Imbert of Focus. Wood-
burning fire. Can be fixed,
pivoted, wall-mounted
or centrally suspended.
Black/grey-painted
8mm (½in) thick steel;
fire aperture (Diameter)
420mm (16½in).
www.focus-creation.com

←

Shaker by Antonio Citterio.
Wood-burning chimney
stove, part of the Fireworks
collection from Skantherm.
Black steel. (H) 1035 x
(W) 400–595mm
(41 x 16–23½in).
www.skantherm.de

↑

Vulcania Mobilia by
Alaxa. Fireplace that uses
bioethanol, a smokeless,
gasless, soot-free and ash-
free fuel. Includes wheels
for easy mobility. Stained
oak and brushed steel.
(H) 1000 x (W) 700 x
(D) 460mm (39½ x
28 x 18in).
www.alaxaproducts.com

←

Switch by Marc Veenendaal for EcoSmart. Free-standing, square-shaped fireplace designed to accept EcoSmart flueless burner. Orange, green or white. (H) 949 x (W) 943 x (D) 406mm (37½ x 37 x 16in). www.ecosmartfire.com

↑

Color X by Tubes Radiators. Hot-water radiator and towel rail from the 1X steel series. Tubular elements have 10mm (½in) diameter. Available in horizontal and vertical versions in a wide selection of colours. Vertical: (H) 400–2000 x (W) 100–760mm (16–79 x 4–30in). Horizontal: (H) 100–760mm x (W) 400–2000mm (4–30 x 16–79in). www.tubesradiatori.com

→

Filiofocus by Atelier Dominique Imbert of Focus. Free-standing fireplace. Fire basin can be built into floor or mounted on steel base. Fire screen made of curved fire-resistant glass. Hood and flue made to measure. Fire basin: (Diameter) 1160mm (46in). www.focus-creation.com

→

Milano by Antonia Astori and Nicola De Ponti for Tubes Radiators. Free-standing radiator, part of Elements collection. Can also be wall- or ceiling-mounted. Available in electric or hydraulic versions. Varnished steel with modular elements. Each module: (H) 130 x (W) 26mm (5 x 1in). www.tubesradiatori.com

↓

Abacus by Aeon. Hydraulic radiator. Comprises vertical pipes adorned with sliced spheres. Available in chrome or ruby red. Two sizes: (H) 950–1600 x (W) 460mm (37½–63 x 18in). www.aeon.uk.com

←

Knockonwood by Jaga. Wooden radiator available in nine different wood types (walnut illustrated). Covers finished with scratch-resistant gloss varnish. (H) 300 x (W) 1400 x (D) 128mm (12 x 55 x 5in). www.jagahome heating.co.uk

→

Iguana Circo by Jaga. Free-standing hot-water radiator. Available in various shapes and with a number of accessories as well as in a variety of colours and glossy or satin-matt finishes.
(H) 1800–2400 x (W) 27–37 x (D) 27–37mm (71–94½ x 1–1½ x 1–1½in).
www.jagahome heating.co.uk

←

Bubble by Andrea Crosetta for Antrax. Wood-burning open-hearth fireplace.
(H) 1000 x (W) 1000 x (D) 550mm (39½ x 39½ x 22in).
www.antrax.it

←

Nester Martin R23 by Euroheat. Multi-fuel stove with triple-skin construction ensuring rapid warm-up. Silver (illustrated) or black. (H) 738 x (W) 512 x (D) 416mm (29 x 20½ x 16½in). www.euroheat.co.uk

↓

Parlour by Thelin. Porcelain enamel stove, available in three versions: gas, wood or pellet. Available in ebony black, ivory, teal green, cobalt blue, burgundy red, or rich brown. (H) 1100 x (Diameter) 508mm (43 x 20in). www.thelinco.com

→

Robey's E905 Romeo. Compact wood-burning stove, part of the Piazzetta stoves range in handcrafted majolica. Convected or radiant heat. (H) 700 x (W) 650 x (D) 410mm (28 x 26 x 16in). www.gruppopiazzetta.com

←
Varde Look 1 by Varde Ovne. Wood-burning stove. Can be top- or rear-connected. Colours include black and grey steel. (H) 960 x (W) 480 x (D) 430mm (38 x 19 x 17in). www.vardeovne.dk

↓
Quint by Carsten Gollnick for Skantherm. Wood-burning chimney stove. Black steel, two window panes. (H) 1167 x (W) 500 x (D) 420mm (46 x 20 x 16½in). www.skantherm.de

→

Silver 24K by Ridea.
Hot-water radiator made
with aluminium plate and
available in a variety of
colours and finishes.
(H) 1800 x (W) 500 x
(D) 8mm (71 x 20 x ½in).
www.ridea.it

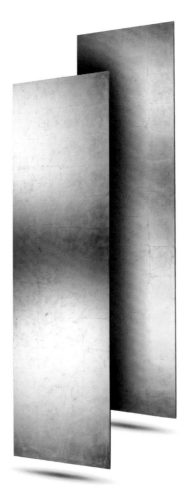

↓

26" by Carlo Magnoli and
Jacco Bregonje for Tubor.
Electric mobile radiator
using the technology
behind flat-screen
televisions and computers.
Aluminium, available with
various finishes. (H) 405 x
(L) 540mm (16 x 21½in).
www.ripples.ltd.uk

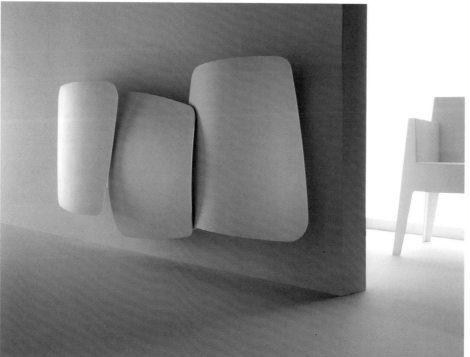

←

Scudi by Massimo Iosa
Ghini for Antrax. Hot-water
radiator available in a
variety of colours. Can be
installed horizontally or
vertically. Steel. (H) 725 x
(W) 1690mm (29 x 67in).
www.antrax.it

↑
Flower Power by Ridea.
Hot-water towel warmer.
Aluminium plate, available
in a variety of colours and
finishes. (Diameter) 600
or 800 x (D) 8mm
(24 or 31½ x ½in).
www.ridea.it

↑
Cheese by Ridea. Hot-
water radiator. Aluminium
plate. Available in a variety
of colours and finishes.
(H) 1500 x (W) 500 x
(D) 8mm (59 x 20 x ½in).
www.ridea.it

←
Garden by Ridea. Hot-
water radiator comprised
of three separate units in
aluminium plate. Available
in a variety of colours
and finishes. Each unit:
(Diameter) 500mm (20in).
www.ridea.it

Towel Rail TV by
Aquavision. Heated screen
prevents misting. All units
come with integrated FM
tuners and fully waterproof
remote control. Ice-white
surround, chrome-finish
waterproof 430mm (17in)
TV screen/mirror. Available
in electric or dual-fuel
versions. (H) 800 x
(W) 500mm (31½ x 20in).
www.aquavision.co.uk

The Spinnaker by
Radiating Style. Hot-water
radiator in tubular steel.
Standard white but other
colours available. (H) 1800
x (W) 600 x (D) 75mm
(71 x 24 x 3in).
www.radiatingstyle.com

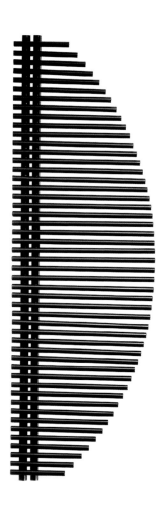

←

Come Round by Eskimo.
Steel radiator, part of the
Outline range. Hot-water or
electric versions available
in a range of colours and
metal finishes. (Diameter)
800mm (31½in).
www.eskimodesign.co.uk

←

You Square by Eskimo. Steel radiator, available in both hot-water and electric versions in a variety of colours and metal finishes. Shallow or deep sizes available. Various dimensions: (H) 600, 800 or 1000 x (W) 600, 800 or 1000mm (24, 31½ or 39½ x 24, 31½ or 39½in). www.eskimodesign.co.uk

↑

Scan DSA 6 by Krog Iversen for Scan. Wood-burning stove, available in black steel with decorative glass. (H) 703 x (W) 470 x (D) 462mm (28 x 18½ x 18in). www.scan.dk

←

Scan DSA 5 by Krog-Iversen for Scan. Free-standing fireplace in black, grey and stainless steel. (H) 1642 x (W) 774 x (D) 608mm (65 x 30½ x 24in). www.scan.dk.

→

System_1 by Studio Dell'Acqua-Bellavitis for Deltacalor. Hot-water radiator, part of the Hit Line collection. Chrome steel, available in three sizes. (H) 950 x (W) 470–1280mm (37 x 18½–50½in). www.deltacalor.com

↑

Raven by Radiant. Brushed stainless-steel radiator. (H) 500 x (W) 1700 x (D) 220mm (20 x 67 x 87in). www.radiant-radiators.co.uk

↑

Creatherm by Arbonia. Curved steel hot-water radiator that doubles as floor-to-ceiling room divider. Available in a range of sizes and colours. (H) 350–2000 x (L) 228–3952mm (14–79 x 9–156in). www.arbonia.com

 ← ↓

Add-On by Satyendra Pakhale for Tubes Radiators. Radiator from Elements collection. Modular concept allows maximum flexibility. Available in electric and hot-water hydraulic versions. Basic component aluminium module: (H) 120 x (W) 240mm (5 x 9½in). www.tubesradiatori.com

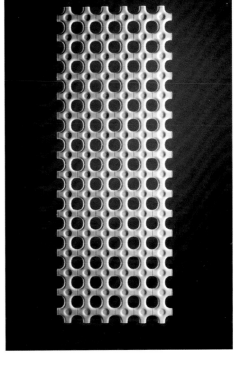

←

Montecarlo by Peter Jamieson for Tubes Radiators. Chrome bathroom radiator from Elements collection. Shelf unit and towel holder combined. Available in horizontal, vertical and square versions. Square version (shown here): (H) 500 x (W) 500mm (20 x 20in). www.tubesradiatori.com

←

Karotherm by Arbonia. Steel radiator, effective horizontally, vertically or as a room divider. Hot-water or electric versions. Available in a large selection of colours. Vertical model (illustrated): (H) 360–2500mm x (W) 300–900 (12–35½ x 14–98½in). Special sizes also available. www.arbonia.com

↓

Rimorchietto by Tubes Radiators. Transportable electric radiator on wooden wheels from Extras collection. Steel construction available in two versions with different widths. (H) 670 x (W) 930 or 960mm (26½ x 37 or 38in). www.tubesradiatori.com

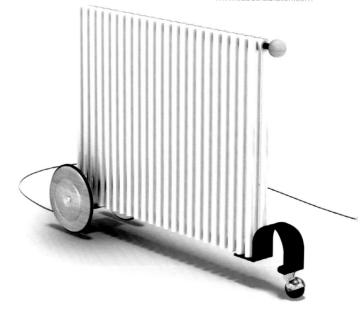

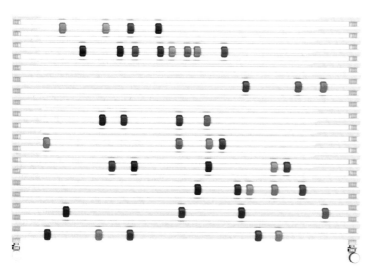

←

Pallottoliere by Francesco Andreazza for Tubes Radiators. Steel radiator from Extras collection. Hydraulic hot-water radiator with white steel pipework and rings, available in a variety of monochromatic and multi-chromatic versions. (H) 640, 720, 800 or 880 x (W) 1200mm (25, 28½, 31½ or 35 x 47½in). www.tubesradiatori.com

←

Retro by Paul Cohen and Marc Veenendaal for EcoSmart. Free-standing fire. Fibreglass, stainless steel and toughened glass. Suitable for indoor and outdoor use. Available in black, royal blue, apple green, signal red, light orange, canary yellow or bright white. Requires no installation. (H) 878 x (W) 880 x (D) 581mm (35 x 35 x 23in). www.ecosmartfire.com

→

Zana-Libra by Frederik Aerts for Thermic Designer Radiators. Steel radiator. Horizontal and vertical versions available in approximately 100 colours. (H) 900, 1400 or 1800 x (L) 384, 464 or 544mm (35, 55 or 71 x 15, 18½ or 21½in). www.thermic.be

↑

Yucca Asymmetrical by
Acova Radiators. Steel.
Available as central-
heating radiator or oil-filled
electric radiator. Finished
in chrome or various
colours. (H) 1736 x
(W) 378mm (68½ x 15in)
and other sizes.
www.acova.co.uk

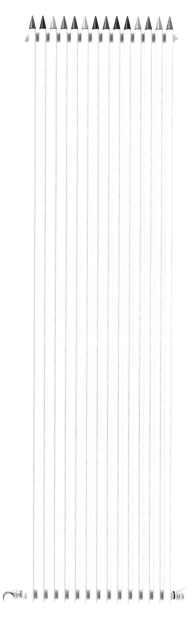

→

Matitone or 'Big Pencil'
by Francesco Andreazza
for Tubes Radiators. Hot-
water radiator from Extras
collection. Tubular steel in
white with coloured caps;
other colour combinations
available on request.
(H) 1400–2000 x
(L) 350–530mm
(55–79 x 14–21in).
www.tubesradiatori.com

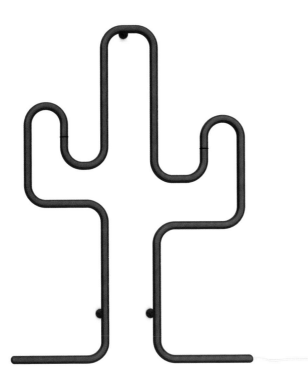

←

Cactus by Tubes Radiators. Electric towel heater from Extras collection. Constructed of steel pipe. Green. (H) 880 x (W) 650mm (35 x 26in). www.tubesradiatori.com

↓

Smeg Retro. Flueless gas fire in stainless steel and glass. Minimum room size 30 cubic metres (1060 cubic feet). Available in red, black, cream or silver. (H) 55 x (W) 800 x (D) 186mm (22 x 31½ x 7½in). www.smeguk.com

↑
Big One by Stafano Ragaini for Ad Hoc, a division of Gruppo Ragaini. Aluminium hot-water radiator. Available in sizes up to (H) 4000mm (160in).
www.grupporagaini.it

→
Electric radiator cum decorative screen by Franca Lucarelli and Bruno Rapisarda for Decor by Scirocco. Brushed stainless steel in three different designs. (H) 1900 x (W) 1200 x (D) 400mm (75 x 47 x 16in).
www.sciroccoh.it

→
VU by Massimo Iosa Ghini for Antrax. Hot-water radiator, shown here as three units combined. Steel plate laser-cut to create flame-like shape. Choice of 200 colours. (H) 1680 x (W) 275mm (66 x 11in).
www.antrax.it

←

Zero-Otto by Francesco Lucchese for Antrax. Aluminium hot-water radiator, available as single or double element. Colours as shown. (Diameter) 800mm (31½in). www.antrax.it

↓

Drop fireplace by Massimo Iosa Ghini for Antrax. Laser-cut varnished steel. (H) 1500 x (W) 1130 x (D) 530mm (59 x 44½ x 21in). www.antrax.it

→

**Saturn and Moon
Radiator** by Peter Rankin
for Antrax. Hidden valves
and controls make the
disks appear to float
across the wall's surface.
Available in hot-water and
electric versions in a variety
of colours. (Diameter)
660mm (26in).
www.antrax.it

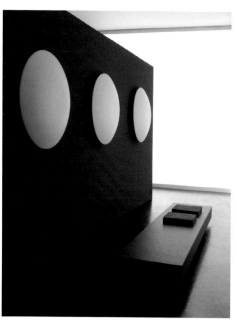

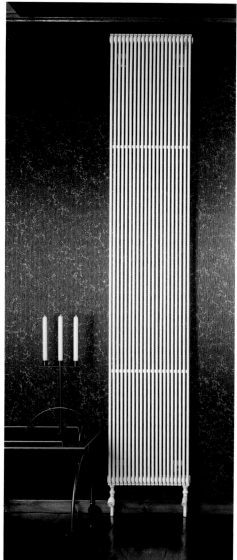

←

Square by Palomba
Serafini for Tubes
Radiators. Radiator from
Elements collection. Ultra-
thin steel, invisible valves,
concealed connections.
Electric or hot-water and
vertical or horizontal
versions available in a wide
variety of dimensions and
colours. Model shown:
(H) 1400 x (W) 810 x
(D) 15mm (55 x 32 x ½in).
www.tubesradiatori.com

↑

Striane by Acova
Radiators. Steel central-
heating radiator. (H) 500–
2000 x (L) 500–3000mm
(20–79 x 20–118in). Can
also be made to measure.
www.acova.co.uk

←

Snake by Franca Lucarelli and Bruna Rapisarda for Scirocco. Hot-water radiator made from stainless steel in either chrome or brushed-steel finish. Electric version also available. (H) 710 x (L) 500mm (28 x 20in). www.sciroccoh.it

↓

Lie Down by Eskimo. Steel radiator, part of the Outline range. Available in hot-water or electric versions in a variety of colours and metal finishes. (H) 240 or 430 x (W) 1000, 1500 or 2000mm (9½ or 17 x 39½, 59 or 79in). www.eskimodesign.co.uk

→

Blade by Peter Rankin for Antrax. Hot-water radiator in extruded aluminium. Available in a variety of colours and special finishes. (H) 1700 x (W) 250mm (67 x 10in). www.antrax.it

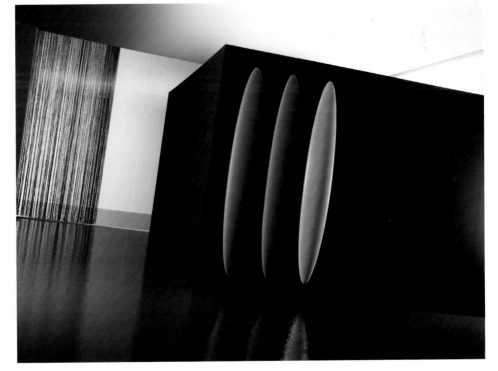

↑
Coil by Cathy Azria for B+D Designs. Steel gas-fired sculptural fireplace with concealed gas burner. Made to measure. www.bd-designs.co.uk

↑
Hot Box by MHS. Hot-water radiator in brushed stainless steel. Range includes matching hot shelf. (H) 350 x (W) 500 x (D) 300mm (14 x 20 x 12in). www.mhsradiators.com

←

Scan DSA E400/E405 by Scan. Wood-burning stove covered in light concrete, in black or grey. (H) 1240 x (W) 920 x (D) 530mm (49 x 36½ x 21in). www.scan.dk

↓

Quadra by Ridea. Hot-water radiator. Four separate units in aluminium plate. Available in a variety of colours and finishes. (H) 500 x (W) 500 x (D) 7mm (20 x 20 x ½in). www.ridea.it

↓

Bonfire 1 by Cathy Azria for B+D Designs. Steel gas-fired sculptural fireplace installation. Made to measure. www.bd-designs.co.uk

→

Movie by Mariano Moroni for the Cordivari Human Living collection. Hot-water radiator in painted carbon steel. Various colours. (H) 1500 x (W) 500mm (59 x 20in). www.cordivari.it

←

Gaya by Roderick Vos for Safretti. Wall-mounted flueless fire, fuelled by bio-alcohol. Stainless steel. (H) 735 x (W) 625 x (D) 150mm (29 x 25 x 6in). www.safretti.com

↑

Hand by Mariano Moroni for the Cordivari Human Living collection. Hot-water radiator in painted carbon steel. Various colours. (H) 1500 x (W) 500mm (59 x 20in). www.cordivari.it

← **Cheese B** by Ridea. Hot-water radiator. Aluminium plate. Available in a variety of colours and finishes. (H) 1500 x (W) 500 x (D) 8mm (59 x 20 x ½in). www.ridea.it

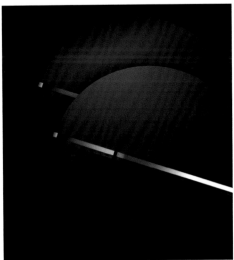

← **Eclisse** by Ridea. Hot-water radiator. Aluminium plate. Available in a variety of colours and finishes. (Diameter) 800mm (31½in). www.ridea.it

↑ **Hole** by Ridea. Hot-water radiator. Aluminium plate. Available in a variety of colours and finishes. (H) 1800 x (W) 500 x (D) 7mm (71 x 20 x ½in). www.ridea.it

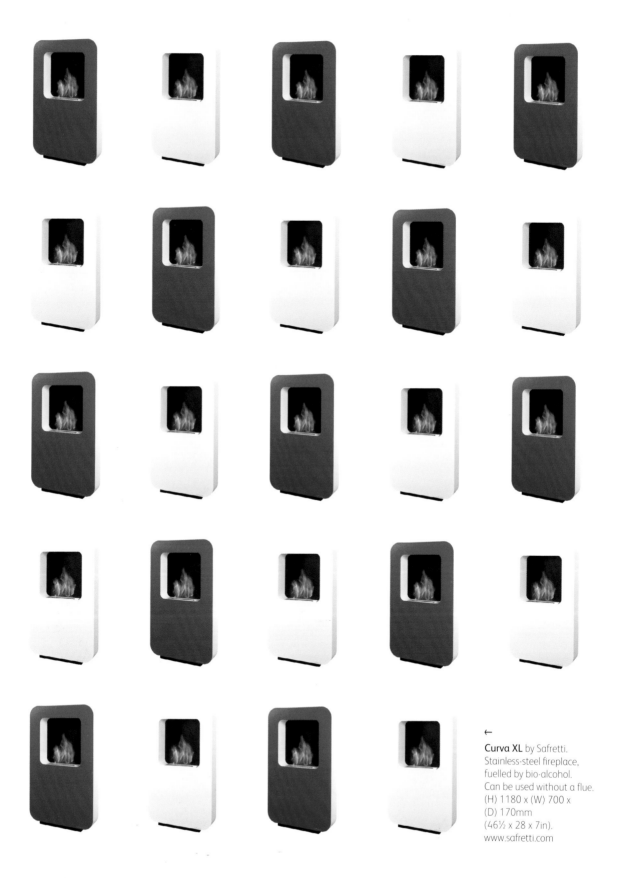

←

Curva XL by Safretti.
Stainless-steel fireplace,
fuelled by bio-alcohol.
Can be used without a flue.
(H) 1180 x (W) 700 x
(D) 170mm
(46½ x 28 x 7in).
www.safretti.com

Kyos by Officina Delle Idee. Hot-water radiator. Sculpture range. Half-mirror/half-steel panel with panels in a wide range of colours or iridescent finishes. Can be supplied without mirror. (H) 1909 x (W) 961 x (D) 35mm (75½ x 38 x 1½in). www.officina-delle-idee.com

↓

Space heater by Naoto Fukasawa for Plus Minus Zero. Oil-filled. Available in red, forest green, baby blue and grey. (H) 300 x (W) 290 x (D) 115mm (12 x 11½ x 4½in). www.plusminuszero.jp

←

Darwin modular wood-burning stove by Sikken. Includes six different furniture elements to use in conjunction with stove. Anthracite-painted steel, and beech wood. (H) 1360 x (W) 350 x (D) 467mm (53½ x 14 x 18½in). www.sikken.ch

↑

Taos by Ruegg-Cheminee.
Pellet stove. Up to 32kg
(76lb) of pellets can be
placed inside the chamber.
Automatic timer, touch-
button controls. Milled
steel or soapstone front
panelling. (H) 1040 x
(W) 560 x (D) 580mm
(50 x 22 x 23in).
www.ruegg-cheminee.com

→

Ray by Sikken. Stove
radiator that doubles as
a hot oven suitable for
cooking pizza. Comfortable
enough to sit on, yet will
warm a large room. Colour
as shown. (H) 885 x
(W) 550 x (D) 648mm
(35 x 22 x 26in).
www.sikken.ch

← **Forma B** by Officina Delle Idee. Hot-water radiator for vertical or horizontal use. Tubular steel, available in a wide colour range, including satin black, satin bronze, tobacco brown, pearl white and pearl grey. Iridescent finishes on request. Each panel (H) 1804 x (W) 200 x (D) 30mm (71 x 8 x 1in). www.officina-delle-idee.com

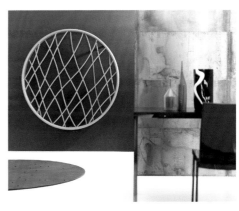

← **Lune** by Officina Delle Idee. Hot-water radiator in tubular and sheet steel. Can be supplied with the radiating panel and tubular pipes in a variety of different colour combinations, including iridescent finishes. (H) 1843 x (W) 590mm (73 x 23½in). www.officina-delle-idee.com

↑ **Medusa** by Officina Delle Idee. Hot-water radiator in various colours, including iridescent finishes. (Diameter) 1415mm (56in). www.officina-delle-idee.com

↓ →

Immagina by Officina Delle Idee. Hot-water radiator. Can be painted after installation with customized colours and designs to blend with decoration. (H) 1800 x (W) 500 x (D) 70mm (71 x 20 x 3in). www.officina-delle-idee.com

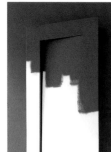

←

Loft by Andrea Crosetta for Antrax. Can be installed horizontally or vertically with up to three elements placed side by side. Aluminium with surface of textured waves. (H) 1500, 1700 or 2000mm (59, 67 or 79in). Single element: (W) 200mm (8in). www.antrax.it

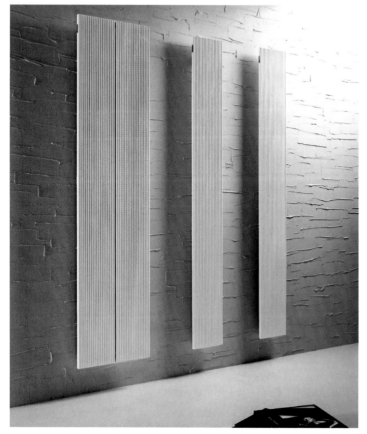

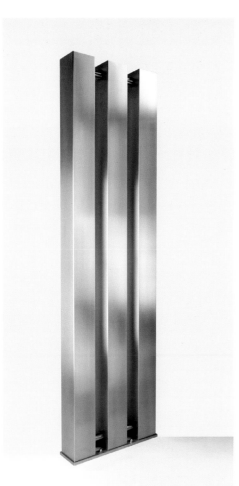

←

Trio by Accuro-Korle. Free-standing, hot-water radiator in stainless steel. (H) 1510 x (W) 439 x (D) 110mm (59½ x 17½ x 4½in). www.accuro-korle.com

↓

Ace by Accuro-Korle. Hot-water, wall-mounted radiator in stainless steel. (H) 590 x (W) 2100 x (D) 30mm (23½ x 83 x 1in). www.accuro-korle.com

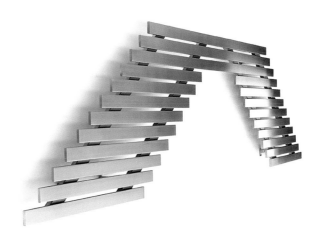

→

Quadraqua by Officina Delle Idee. Shelf radiator available in various colours and iridescent finishes. (H) 1120 or 1830 x (W) 150 x (D) 150mm (44 or 72 x 6 x 6in). www.officina-delle-idee.com

→

Grado by Officina Delle Idee. Hot-water radiator in steel tube. Colours include satin black, satin bronze, tobacco brown, pearl white and pearl grey. (H) 1834 x (W) 600 x (D) 30mm (72½ x 24 x 1in). www.officina-delle-idee.com

↓

X-Front by Attika. Wood-burning stove in marble, sandstone or granite with plain or coated steel. Available in two colours: slate or platinum. Firebox: (H) 430 x (W) 550 x (D) 360mm (17 x 22 x 14in). www.attika.ch

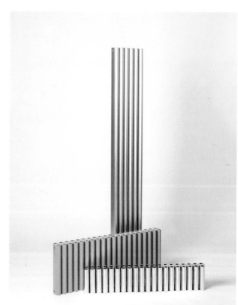

↑

Ron by Eskimo. Electrical radiator. Modular system of elliptical tubes in polished or matt aluminium or any colour required. Available in six sizes. (H) 200–2000mm (8–79in). www.eskimodesign.co.uk

→

GEO by Attika. Wood-burning stove that releases gentle heat continuously for fifteen hours through the stone of the fireplace. Soapstone and ceramic glass. Firebox: (H) 430 x (W) 315 x (D) 315mm (17 x 12½ x 12½in). www.attika.ch

↑

Pilar by Attika. Wood-burning
fire. Cylindrical design with
glass door. Available in steel
platinum or steel quartz
colours. Firebox: (H) 475 x
(W) 275 x (D) 245mm
(19 x 11 x 10in).
www.attika.ch

Chapter four

KITCHENS

→

Norbert Wangen

Norbert Wangen is in the vanguard of those designers who in the 1990s began to break free from the constraints of the traditional kitchen to evolve a new aesthetic. His compact creations are as far removed from traditional kitchen design as it is possible to get. Wangen became interested in kitchens while studying to be an architect. His designs – from the seminal K4 of 1994, with its sliding, extending top, to the K14 of 2008, with its mechanized opening systems and remote controls – reflect a process of continual refinement. The K4 kitchen was so ahead of its time that Wangen initially had problems finding a company to manufacture it. That K4 could still be described today as avant-garde is a tribute to the designer's vision. K4 is a monoblock structure with a sliding top that closes to conceal storage for kitchen essentials. Wangen's streamlined designs are not for those who hanker after a cosy hearth with a singing kettle. These kitchens offer no compromise; there is no attempt to soften their austerity. Wangen creates sculptural objects, whose forms are seamless and whose functions are skilfully hidden.

In 2003 Wangen's eponymous kitchen and bathroom business, based in Switzerland, was bought by the Italian company Boffi, for which he continues to design today. For Wangen, kitchens have an enduring appeal. 'The kitchen is one of the most important rooms in the house,' he says. 'We spend a great deal of our lives in the kitchen, as research shows. I designed my first kitchen in 1994, and when I go back to that time and look at what kitchen manufacturers were producing, it appears to me that they were only interested in handles – boxes with handles.' For Wangen to produce a kitchen with a sliding top represented some sort of revolution. 'At the outset, it was not a real kitchen, just a concept. It didn't look like a traditional kitchen any more – a traditional kitchen in the sense of a workshop for food preparation. It was more like a piece of refined functional elegance whose functions were hidden.' Wangen's designs are self-contained studies in economy and detail, featuring gliding mechanisms and inventive lighting elements, while the purification system employed in the K11 and K12 kitchens are so effective that no external vent is required.

Wangen would be the first to argue that the way we use our kitchens has changed dramatically since the 1950s. 'In the past, people sat and ate together,' he says. 'They spent a great deal of time in the kitchen preparing meals. Not so today – we are in a new epoch.'

Today, the once rigid demarcation lines between the kitchen and living room have disappeared, giving way to one large open-plan space, better suited to our casual lifestyles; bathroom and bedroom boundaries are blurring in the same way. The way we prepare meals has changed. What we eat has changed. The way we wash dishes and deal with our waste has changed. Eating is a much more informal affair than it used to be, often requiring no more preparation than opening a packet of food and operating a microwave oven. The kitchen is becoming smaller, often reduced to one single element, and yet, despite its size, it remains the nucleus of the home, the metaphorical hearth. Wangen believes that large kitchens are superfluous. 'A professional cook requires very little space to prepare food,' he says. 'I don't think these huge kitchens fulfil a genuine need.'

A master of materials and form, Wangen displays a craftsman's sensitivity to the construction process. It comes as no surprise to learn that his father was a carpenter who made furniture. 'I also made furniture and objects,' says Wangen, 'and in the process I became interested in sculpture.' It could be said that he still makes furniture, albeit of an industrial genre. 'I attended the Academy of Sculpture at Düsseldorf,' says Wangen, 'and found a teacher, Attila Kotányi, who taught me about abstract art. From Attila I acquired an anarchistic and radical approach [to design].' Kotányi – who had been a member of the Situationists, a political and artistic group based in Paris in the 1960s – has had a lasting influence on Wangen, who remains deeply interested in the abstract. Indeed, such was his acknowledged debt to Kotányi that Wangen named one of his early pieces of furniture the Attila Armchair. Wangen also studied philosophy and worked in set design. 'For me, it was a personal goal to experience a lot of things. I ended up in a very specialized area of design. I've worked on many levels in many dimensions to reach this point.'

Wangen has a philosophical approach to design and believes that anything is possible. 'A sense of limitation fences you in,' he says. 'In our case, a design product has various aspects and dimensions – cultural, aesthetical, commercial – that might contradict each other. A good solution should bring everything together by convincing and not by compromising. Even if this is an ideal image, we have to be aware of where we are and what we are doing – not simply reacting to extraneous forces.'

Wangen has some useful advice for anyone contemplating a new kitchen. 'You must think hard about what you really need and how you can create a kitchen that suits your lifestyle. Avoid clichés. You should also give yourself plenty of time to work things out,' he says, 'Remember that a good professional cook can produce a good meal in a space the size of a broom cupboard.' Wangen believes that good design is enduring: 'The K2 still looks as good today as it did in 2000. I want to take people away from the slavish pursuit of fashion.'

This is a view that will find a lot of support in today's highly disposable society.

←

Open & Closed
monoblock compact kitchen unit by Sheer (see page 182).

→

Banco by Luca Meda for Dada. Worktop incorporates hob and sink. Futura wall unit houses built-in appliances. Available in steel, Corian and aluminium in a range of colours.
www.dadaweb.it

↑

SC112 multifunction oven by Smeg from the Linear series. Full frameless glass front, violet backlight. (H) 597 x (W) 597 x (D) 545mm (24 x 24 x 21½in).
www.smeguk.com

←

Zone kitchen by Piero Lissoni for Boffi. Modular system with base units equipped with sliding doors. Available in a free-standing island or wall version with plinths in stainless steel. Doors available in setasil, polyester, M+ (matt plus), wood veneer and aluminium. Recessed handles in stainless steel with satin finish.
www.boffi.it

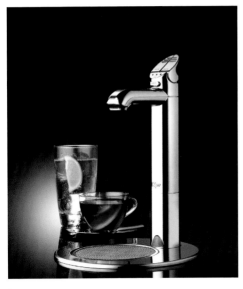

↓
Continua by Paolo Nava and Fabio Casiraghi for Binova. Thin shelves and concealed lights emphasize the floating base design. Wide range of colours and configurations available in high-gloss lacquer, matt lacquer, veneer and aluminium. www.binova.it

↑
Hydro tap by Zip UK. Instant boiling and chilled filtered water from a single tap. Range of sizes and options available. Chromed brass. (H) 334 x (W)188 x (D) 320mm (13 x 7½ x 12½in). wwwzipheaters.co.uk

←
Dominia kitchen by Aster Cucine. Retro-influenced design in laminate and steel. Available in forty lacquered colours as well as natural wood. Features integrated LED lighting. www.astercucine.com

→

KV1 mixer tap by Arne Jacobsen for Vola. Solid stainless-steel version of design classic. Single-handle mixer with ceramic disc technology (instead of rubber washers) and double-swivel spout in stainless steel and ceramic. Available in polished chrome or range of fourteen colours. (H) 235 x (D) 200mm (9½ x 8in). www.vola.dk

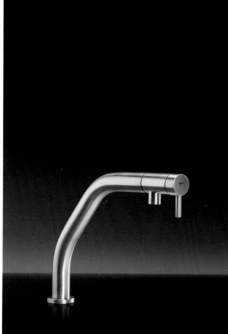

↑

Nemo by MGS Progetti. Single-hole mixer tap with pull-out hose. Solid stainless steel, ceramic. (H) 227 x (D) 307mm (9 x 12½in). www.mgsprogetti.com

→

Wood 100 % kitchen by Giancarlo Vegni for Effeti. Single block of varnished chestnut handcrafted by Tarpac of Lucca, Italy. Available in various dimensions. www.effeti.com

↓
Evoke kitchen tap with pull-out spray by Kohler. Three-function spray head with 360-degree spout rotation. Made of steel, ceramic and nylon. Available in chrome, nickel or stainless steel finishes. (H) 287 x (D) 229mm (11½ x 9in). www.kohler.com

↑
500T1 by Vola. Single-lever hand shower in solid stainless steel and ceramic with 2m (79in) extendable hose. (H) 83 x (D) 200mm (3½ x 8in). www.vola.dk

→
Prologue single sink with wet surface area by Kohler. Left- and right-hand versions available. Stainless steel. Various sizes. www.kohler.com

←
Biofuel-ready Aga oven
by Rayburn. Runs on
natural or propane gas,
oil or electricity and, with
minor modifications,
biofuels. Cast iron with
enamel finish in wide
range of colours. (H) 851
x (W) 1487 x (D) 679mm
(33½ x 59 x 27in).
www.aga-web.co.uk

→
Concept 40 kitchen by
Leicht. Linear format with
concealed details and
storage. Steel laminate.
Available in various finishes
and colours.
www.leicht.de

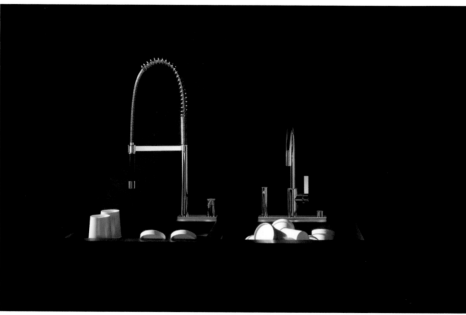

←
Kitchen Zones cleaning
set by Sieger Design for
Dornbracht. Tara Ultra
two-hole mixer with Profi
spray and cover plate; Tara
Ultra single-lever mixer
with strainer waste and
control handle. Integrated
washing-up liquid
dispenser and cover plate.
Steel, composite plastic
with chrome and platinum
matt finish. Various
dimensions.
www.dornbracht.de

↑

Nuova by Minotti. Entire kitchen is made of stone. Available in a variety of stone finishes and configurations. Marble and Latti veneer.
www.minotticucine.it

→

T45 by MGS Progetti. Three-hole kitchen mixer with pull-out spout from the T45 Collection. Solid stainless steel, also available in shiny finish. (H) 350 x (D) 180mm (14 x 7in).
www.mgsprogetti.com

← ↑

Cinqueterre kitchen by Vico Magistretti for Schiffini. First kitchen to be constructed entirely in aluminium. Anodized aluminium doors feature wave-shaped profile. Wall, base and island units available in aluminium or sliding glass. Natural or black finish. www.schiffini.it

Unit Cubic compact
kitchen by Rieber. Includes
water and extraction
points. Steel and laminate.
Available in various finishes
and dimensions.
www.rieber.de

→

Waterstation Round
by Max Maier for Rieber.
Compact modular kitchen
system in stainless steel.
Available in various
configurations with a
range of additional units
and frames. (H) 920–1000
x (Diameter) 900mm
(36½–39½ x 35½in).
www.rieber.de

↓

DF6 FAB by Smeg. Steel 1950s-style free-standing dishwasher. Energy rating: AAA. Available in eight colours, including lime green (shown). (H) 885 x (W) 590 x (D) 641mm (32 x 24 x 25½in). www.smeg.com

←

J-Series Side-by-Side refrigerator by Jasper Morrison for Samsung. Dual-zone cooling; energy-saving home-bar feature allows access to items without opening the door. Available in various finishes including stainless steel. (H) 1775 x (W) 912 x (D) 672mm (70 x 36 x 27in). www.samsung.com

→

400 series wine storage by Sub-Zero. Reds and whites can be stored in separate temperature zones. Various configurations and refrigerator combinations available. Glass, steel, rustproof wire, natural cherrywood. (H) 2134 x (W) 762 x (D) 610mm (84 x 30½ x 24in). www.subzero.com

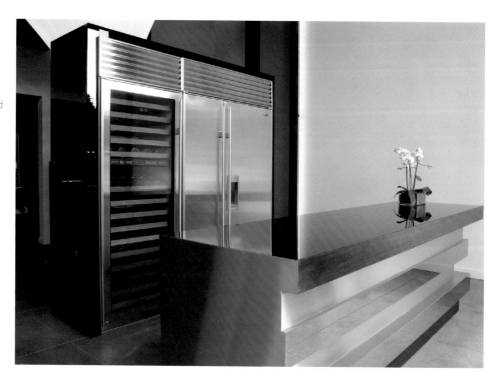

←

JLTDC10 condenser tumble dryer by John Lewis. A-rated energy-saving dryer. Pared-down design uses the latest heat-pump technology to ensure energy efficiency; requires no plumbing or venting. Steel. (H) 850 x (W) 600 x (D) 600mm (33½ x 24 x 24in). www.johnlewis.com

→

GR-G267ATBA TV side-by-side refrigerator by LG. Features 38cm (13in) LCD, TV, DVD player and radio with remote control. Titanium silver finish. (H) 1751 x (W) 894 x (D) 790mm (69 x 35½ x 31½in). www.lge.com

↑

Art side-by-side refrigerator by LG. Features decorative floral pattern with optional addition of Swarovski crystals. Stainless steel. (H) 1758 x (W) 898 x (D) 702mm (69½ x 35½ x 28in). www.lge.com

←

File kitchen storage system by Pietro Arosio for Ernestomeda. Storage system designed to complement the Solaris system. Steel with matt-black lacquer finish. www.ernestomeda.com

→

Functional shelves by Alno. Striking appearance provided by glass backboards in a variety of colours with integrated downlights. Aluminium and glass. Available in various dimensions. www.alno.de

← **You** customizable fridge freezer by Brastemp. Several thousand possible colour combinations. Options include separate temperature zones and glass-chilling unit. (H) 1868 x (W) 710 x (D) 711mm (73½ x 28 x 28in) www.brastemp.com

← **Wine Cooler** by Samsung. Holds twenty-nine bottles. Electronic temperature control, digital LED display. (H) 838 x (W) 508 x (D) 584mm (33 x 20 x 23in). www.samsung.com

↓ **430** glass-fronted refrigerator for wine storage by Sub-Zero. Each compartment has independent temperature control. Stainless steel and glass. (H) 1854 x (W) 910 x (D) 610mm (73 x 36 x 25in). www.subzero.com

→

b3 functional boxes by Bulthaup. Integrated accessories to complement the b3 system. Invisible storage system frees up valuable workspace. Glass-fronted with integrated fluorescent lighting. (H) 630 x (W) 600 x (D) 120mm (25 x 24 x 5in). www.bulthaup.com

↓

b1 kitchen by Bulthaup. Pared down to the essential elements. Range includes wall and island units. Available in a variety of wood and coloured laminates. www.bulthaup.com

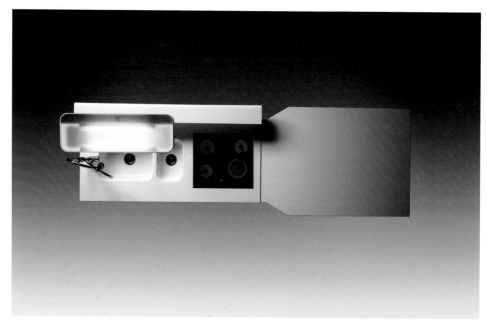

←

Solaris free-standing kitchen by Pietro Arosio for Ernestomeda. Includes tap, sink, hob, lighting and drawer unit. Corian, glass and steel. (H) 900 x (L) 3330 x (D) 800mm (35½ x 130 x 31½in). www.ernestomeda.com

←

MODE kitchen storage system by Pietro Arosio for Ernestomeda. Includes oven column, dishwasher and refrigerator with freezer. Gloss lacquer, aluminium, steel. www.ernestomeda.com

↓

700 series integrated refrigerator system by Sub-Zero. Fridge or freezer units can be incorporated into island or wall configurations. Steel and laminate. Unit dimensions: (H) 2032 x (W) 686 x (D) 610mm (80 x 27 x 24in). www.subzero.com

b1/b3 slatted extractor hood by Herbert H. Schultes for Bulthaup. Sculptural design in aluminium. (W) 900–1200 x (D) 600 mm (35½–47½ x 24in). www.bulthaup.com

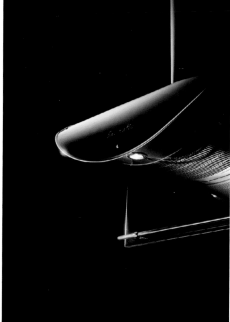

↑
Solari AS17 by Alberto Solari for Baumatic. Chimney hood from the Studio Solari collection. Stainless steel featuring integrated utensil-holder and lighting. (H) Min. 945 x (W) 900 x (D) 425mm (37½ x 35½ x 17in). www.baumatic.com

←
Reflex kitchen by Marco Pareschi for Scavolini. Sturdy wood. Lacquered finishes in a variety of colours or glass. Well-equipped worktops and roomy storage units. www.scavolini.com

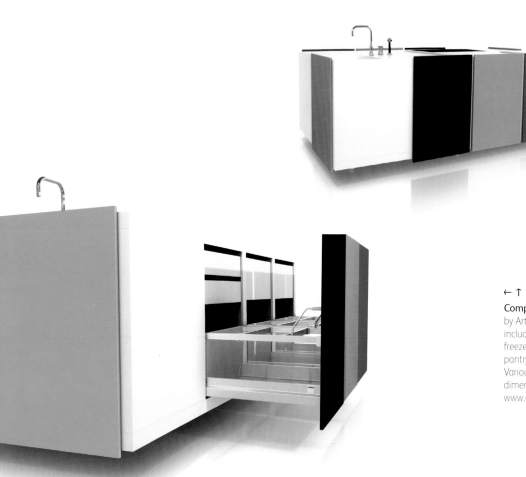

← ↑
Compacta kitchen island
by Artificio. Storage section
includes refrigerator,
freezer, cool box and
pantry. Acrylic and steel.
Various colours and
dimensions.
www.artificio.es

→
Futura downdraft vent,
part of the Cielo line by
Exklusiv-Hauben Guttman
GmbH. Hood slides into
worktop with the press of
a button. Stainless steel
and glass. (H) 500 x
(W) 900–1200mm
(20 x 35½–47½in).
www.gutmann-exklusiv.eu

→ ↓
Open & Closed

monoblock compact kitchen unit by Sheer. The two hemispheres retract and fold to reveal a fully equipped kitchen with a range of appliances and accessories. The free-standing wall unit with motorized shutter contains a pull-out table and chairs. Steel, aluminium, Corian. (Diameter) 1480mm (58½in).
www.sheer.it

↑
Long Island cooking table by Andi Kern for Alno. Free-standing cooking table combines fixed cooking block with an inlaid table, which can move either side of the base frame. Stainless steel, wood veneer or laminate. Tabletop available in a variety of wood finishes. Cooking block: (H) 818 x (W) 1000 x (D) 620mm (32½ x 39½ x 24½in). Tabletop: (W) 850 x (L) 2200mm (33½ x 87in). www.alno.de

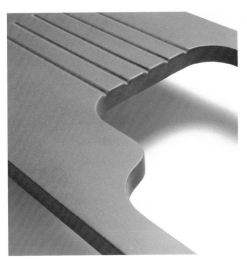

←

Mass concrete worktop material by Cast Advances Concretes. Smooth, heat-proof, stain-proof and lighter than stone or standard concrete. A natural product that can be made to measure in a wide variety of colours. www.massconcrete.co.uk

→

Venus kitchen by Pinninfarina Design for Snaidero. Comes in a variety of gloss, matt lacquers and wood finishes as well as Microtouch, a leather-like finish. Photograph shows high-gloss lacquer in coral red. www.snaidero.com

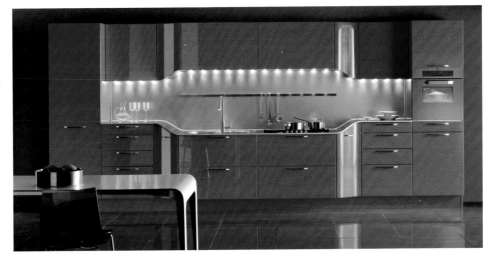

←

Tivali enclosed monoblock kitchen by Dante Bonuccelli for Dada. Compact kitchen designed as a single wall unit or stand-alone item. Stainless steel, extruded aluminium, laminate. www.dadaweb.it

→

Bridge kitchen by Giorgio Armani for Armani Casa. Sukupira wood frame, woven bronze or bronze glass doors, ground quartz worktops. Features island unit with free-standing wall units.
www.armanicasa.it

←

Onda kitchen by Rational. Features curved surfaces and specially developed extractor hood. Wide range of colours, finishes and units available. Shown here in dark plum lacquer and black glass.
www.rational.de

→

Arwa-Twinflex mixer tap by Florin Baeriswyl for Arwa. Chrome finish. Flexible spout allows water to be directed anywhere. New Trigon mixing technology conserves water. Available in four colours: orange, pigeon blue, beige-grey and black. (H) 380mm (15in).
www.arwa.ch

Flux kitchen by Fabrizio Guigiaro for Scavolini. Range includes circular cooking console and furniture. Available in veneered and lacquered finishes as well as transparent glass with aluminium frames.
www.scavolini.com

↓
The People kitchen by Marconato and Zappa from the Vogue range for Comprex. Smooth, sharp, rectangular forms dominate. Stainless steel, glass and a variety of laminated or veneered finishes available.
www.comprex.it

←

Lot two-hole mixer tap with individual rosettes by Sieger Design for Dornbracht. Also available without rosette. Polished chrome or matt platinum finishes. (Projection) 235mm (9½in). www.dornbracht.com

← ↑

Poker by Luigi Trenti for the Cucina series by Cisal. Single-lever sink mixer with 360-degree rotation in chrome-plated brass. (H) 241mm (10in). www.cisal.it

→

Extra 04 kitchen by MK Cucine. Intricately grained ebony wood featuring 30mm (1¼in)-thick doors. Other combinations available include graphite oak/steel, white gloss/ stone and black gloss/ zebrawood.
www.mkcucine.com

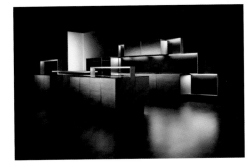

↑ →

P-7340 kitchen by Porsche Design for Poggenpohl. Anodized titanium-coloured aluminium frame. Ultra-thin worktops in satinized glass, quartz or stone. Doors in brushed pine or dark oak. Range includes sideboard, AV unit, customized Miele appliances and table.
www.poggenpohl.de

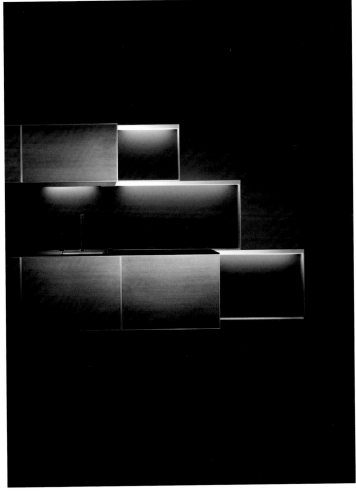

↑

Z.Island Kitchen by Zaha Hadid in collaboration with DuPont Corian and Ernestomeda. Z.Island is a 'sensory-responsive kitchen environment' featuring multimedia equipment, sound actuators and LEDs that enable users to surf the Internet, listen to music or create a particular ambience by means of a centralized touch-control panel. Includes two separate island units: 'Fire' (the cooking area) and 'Water' (the washing area). In addition, a modular cabinet-wall system complements the two islands. Corian. Available by special order only.
www.ernestomeda.com

→

Corian Nouvel Lumieres by Jean Nouvel with DuPont and Ernestomeda. Futuristic kitchen in high-tech materials and finishes. All the elements are in Corian, which appears in a variety of unusual applications including touch-control panels and heating membranes. Cupboard and wall cabinets are translucent panels, supported around the edges by a Plexiglas frame. The backlit rear panels create shadow effects with the shapes of the utensils inside. Appliances by Scholtè.
www.ernestomeda.com

→

**Artematica Vitrum
Arte Kitchen** designed
by Gabriele Centazzo for
Valcucine. Customized
kitchen featuring glass
panels and aluminium
structural frame. Panels in
various materials, including
layered HPL in many
different colours, wood
laminate, lacquered MDF
and glass. Available in
various configurations
and dimensions.
www.valcucine.it

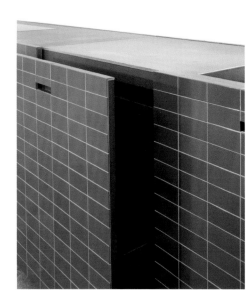

← Tile kitchen by Vincent Van Duysen for Obumex. Specially designed polished ceramic tiles with formed stainless-steel worktop. Modular system for island or wall use. Tiles available in three colours: butter, terracotta and moss green.
www.obumex.be

↑ Xila kitchen by Luigi Massoni for Boffi. Reintroduction of 1972 classic, the first kitchen to be conceived without handles. Laminated wood and aluminium; worktops available in Corian, granite, marble, stone, stainless steel and wood.
www.boffi.com

← Bart Lens kitchen for Obumex. Based on Copenhagen tableware design with digitally printed surface pattern. Island cooking unit with separate wall storage. Laminate and glass.
www.obumex.be

←

RY495 fridge-freezer by Gaggenau. Five alternative storage areas, each with different climate zones. No-frost technology, 'A' rating for energy. Can be designed for free-standing use or partially integrated. Stainless-steel finishes.
(W) 907 x (H) 1740–1760 x (D) 600mm
(36 x 69 x 23½in).
www.gaggenau.com

→

Francesco Ravo kitchen for Obumex. Modular system with two wall units and central island. Corian and high-gloss lacquer MDF in a range of bespoke colours.
www.obumex.be

←

L'Evoluzione by Giancarlo Vegni for Effeti. Dominated by impressive extractor. Lacquer, steel and glass. Available in various materials, finishes and colours.
www.effeti.com

→
Side-by-Side wine cooler/
fridge-freezer by John
Lewis. Stainless steel.
(H) 1855 x (W) 1090 x
(D) 572mm (73 x
43 x 23in).
www.johnlewis.com

↑
Moon washing machine
by Giorgetto Guigaro
for Indesit. Four buttons
to control all washing
requirements. Several
colour options available.
(H) 850 x (W) 595 x
(D) 535mm (33½ x
23 x 21in).
www.indesit.com

→
Gourmet dual-fuel
cooker by Stoves. Seven-
burner gas hob, wok
burner, electric oven
and removable cast-iron
griddle. Stainless steel.
(H) 900 x (W) 1100 x
(D) 600mm (35½ x
43½ x 24½in).
www.stovesranges.co.uk

→

Evolution Emotion by Whirlpool. Decorative cooker hood with ambient lighting. Stainless steel. (H) 510–1300 x (W) 360 x (D) 340mm (20–51 x 14 x 13in). www.whirlpool.co.uk

→

M207 range hood by Sirius. Chunky extractor in brushed stainless steel. (H) 640–1130 x (W) 400 x (D) 400mm (25½–44½ x 16 x 16in). www.siriuscappe.com

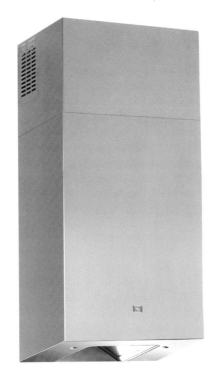

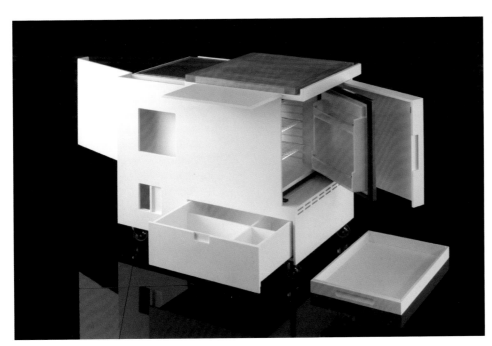

←

Minikitchen by Boffi. Reissue of a 1966 design by Joe Colombo. Compact design deceptively accommodates fridge, hob, chopping board storage drawers and a pull-out work surface. New features include Corian finish, induction hob and additional power sockets. Needs just one power socket to operate. (H) 957 x (W) 1071 x (D) 650mm (38 x 42½ x 26in). www.boffi.com

↑

Ora-Ito kitchen collection by Ito Morabito for Gorenje. The range of sleek black-glass kitchen appliances includes ovens and ceramic hobs, fridges, dishwashers and microwaves. Available in black or black with silver. www.gorenjegroup.com

↓

Barrique kitchen by Ernestomeda. Features brilliant-glass and lacquered cabinets, marble worktop and wine rack. Also available in wide range of alternative finishes and materials, including wood, lacquer, laminate and microline. www.ernestomeda.com

→

Swing extractor hood by Franke. Low-noise extractor with eight-speed soft-touch control. Also available in white glass finish. Stainless steel, glass. (H) 1145–1626 x (W) 898 x (D) 395mm (45–64½ x 35½ x 15½in). www.franke.com

↓
**Starry Night Premium
Touch** fridge freezer by
Gorenje. Features 26,000
Swarovski crystals, touch-
screen control panel and
built-in radio. Black.
(H) 2000 x (W) 600 x
(D) 645mm
(79 x 24 x 25½in).
www.gorenje.com

↑
Blancoadelante 515
extractor hood by
Guttman for Blanco.
Can be custom-made
and matched to any RAL
colour. Stainless steel and
glass. (H) 1100–1500 x
(W) 900 x (D) 450mm
(43½–59 x 35½ x 18in).
www.blanco.com

→

Vario cooktops by Gaggenau. Modular range offering ten special-purpose appliances including extractor, steamer, induction wok and teppanyaki grill. 400 series shown. Stainless steel. (W) 510 x (L) 914 x (D) 130mm (20 x 36 x 5½in). www.gaggenau.com

↑

Planar kitchen sink by Franke. Geometric single-bowl drainer in stainless steel with silk finish. (W) 1000 x (D) 510mm (39½ x 20in). www.franke.com

←

Honeycomb built-in electric cooktop by Kuppersbusch. Flush-fitting, hexagonal components can be configured in up to twenty-eight shapes, ideal for use on island units. Sensor control for six cooking zones. Glass ceramic. (W) 320 x (L) 320mm (13 x 13in). www.kuppersbuschusa.com

→

Waterstation Cubic 600
kitchen sink by Max Maier
for Rieber. Combines
with other elements of
the Rieber Workstation
modular concept.
Stainless steel. (H) 175 x
(W) 600 x (D) 517mm
(7 x 24 x 18in).
www.rieber.de

←

Steam Direct Drive
washing machine with
LCD by LG. First washing
machine to incorporate
steam technology in the
washing process. Limited-
edition Designers Guild
versions shown. (H) 842
x (W) 600 x (D) 600mm
(33½ x 24 x 24in).
www.lge.com

→ **Floral Collection** cooker from Rangemaster. Special edition features bright floral designs and a warming zone. (H) 898–925 x (W) 1092 x (D) 600mm (35½–36 x 43½ x 24in). www.rangemaster.co.uk

↑
Professional Series
open-burner gas range by Viking. Available in a variety of finishes and burner configurations. Stainless-steel body, cast-iron burners. (H) 920–965 x (W) 920 x (D) 635mm (36½–38 x 36½ x 25in). www.vikingrange.com

→

Hi-line modular kitchen
by Ferruccio Laviani
for Dada. Components
available in a variety of
surface and colour finishes.
Includes a special lighting
system. Stainless steel and
extruded aluminium.
www.dadaweb.it

←

Genesi 120 double
oven and hood by Steel.
Stainless steel, cast iron,
enamel. Variety of burner
and grill configurations
available. (H) 900 x
(W) 1172 x (D) 599mm
(35½ x 46½ x 25in).
www.steel-cucine.com

← **Opera** double range cooker by Smeg. Multifunction ovens, ceramic hob, electric griddle. Stainless steel. (H) 900 x (W) 1000 x (D) 600mm (35½ x 39½ x 25in). www.smeg.com

↓ **Competence Teppan Yaki** hob by AEG/Electrolux. High-grade steel surface allows for rapid and even heat distribution. Two grill zones can be controlled independently. Stainless steel. (W) 380 or 580 x (L) 510mm (15 or 23 x 20in). www.aeg-electrolux.co.uk

↑ **Thermastone Heatstore** range cooker by Seymourpowell for Mercury Appliances. Twice the heat storage capacity of cast iron. Unique twist-grip controls. Available in a range of colours. Stainless steel, vitreous enamel, cast iron, silicon carbide. (H) 900 x (W) 1090 x (D) 700mm (35½ x 43 x 28in). www.mercury-appliances.co.uk

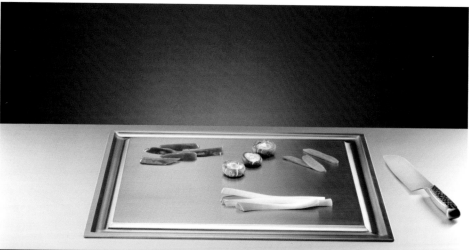

←

KYDEX kitchen by Sietze Kalkwijk for Studio Kalkwijk. Ideal for very small kitchens. Exterior finish is a high-quality thermoplastic called Kydex. (H) 930 x (W) 2000 x (D) 800mm (37 x 79 x 31½in).
www.kalkwijk.com

← ↑

Space cooker hood by Elica. Uses patented technology to reduce noise by 35% compared to standard cooker hoods. Steel and tempered glass. (Diameter) 800mm (31½in).
www.elica.com

→

Works by Piero Lissoni for Boffi. Stainless-steel free-standing kitchen with integrated sink and gas hob, bleached-oak storage units on castors. Wall system in stainless steel and glass with sliding doors. www.boffi.com

↑ →

Elektra kitchen by Pietro Arosio for Ernestomeda. Horizontal overlapping volumes that can be equipped in various ways. Finishes include laminate, lacquer in various colours, stainless steel, marble and Corian. www.ernestomeda.it

↑
Insight cooker hood
by Electrolux. Simple
horizontal design with
electronic touch controls.
Stainless steel, glass.
(H) 900 x (W) 898 x
(D) 310mm (35½ x 35½
x 12½in).
www.electrolux.co.uk

←
Double dish drawer
dishwasher by Fisher &
Paykel. Drawers function
independently, improving
economy by matching
washing programs to
appropriate contents.
Stainless steel or black.
(H) 820–880 x (W) 595
x (D) 570mm (32½–35 x
23½ x 22½in).
www.fisherpaykel.co.uk

←
PLUSMODO by Jorge
Pensi for Poggenpohl.
Architectural kitchen
featuring extra-thick
worktops and glass storage
elements. Aluminium,
glass, wood veneer and
aqua-based satin lacquers.
www.poggenpohl.de

Midway System light panel by Thomas Ritt and Tino Toppler for Miele. Panel is up to 3m (10ft) long and offers even illumination without dazzling the eyes. Coloured stainless steel and glass. (H) 521 x (W) variable x (D) 67mm (20½ x variable x 2½in). www.miele-kuechen.com

Ondus taps by Paul Flowers for Grohe. Digitally controlled with personalized presets. Solid brass with four monochromatic finishes: white, black and chrome and titanium. (H) 216 x (Diameter) 65mm (8½ x 2½in). www.grohe.com

Quooker Modern tap by Quooker. Dispenses filtered boiling water, which is held in an insulated tank below the work surface. Water dispersed in fine spray to prevent burns. Childproof and height-adjustable. Comes in four models with six finishes available. Tap: (H) 320 x (D) 164 x (Diameter) 50mm (12½ x 6½ x 2in). Tank: (H) 400–470 x (Diameter) 150–200mm (16–18½ x 6–8in). www.quooker.com

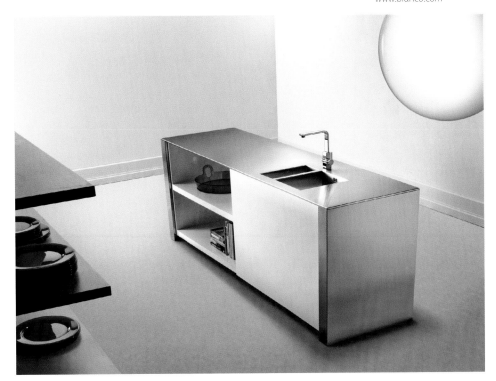

Fassett table by Blanco.
Combines minimalist lines
in steel with chamfered
edges. Can be integrated
or used free-standing.
Made to order.
www.blanco.com

Integration kitchen by
Poggenpohl. Features
high-quality acrylic
materials and woods
paired with aluminium
and glass. Also available
in high-gloss colours,
zebrano, Swiss pear tree
and walnut veneers.
www.poggenpohl.de

← Solitaire Steelart worktop system by Blanco. Modular components can be arranged in a variety of configurations. Stainless-steel sinks, work surfaces and cabinets all made to specification including matching hood. www.blanco.com

↓ b3 monoblock by Bulthaup. Floating kitchen system featuring ultra-thin worktops and multifunctional wall system. Wall-hanging and floor-standing versions available with many elements and accessories. Available in a wide range of materials and finishes. www.bulthaup.com

←

Nomis kitchen by Hannes Wettstein for Dada. Features double-sided work island with formed sink and sunken hob. Range of wall units, counters and storage options makes numerous configurations possible. Stainless steel, extruded aluminium, glass laminate and wood. Other finishes and materials available. www.dadaweb.it

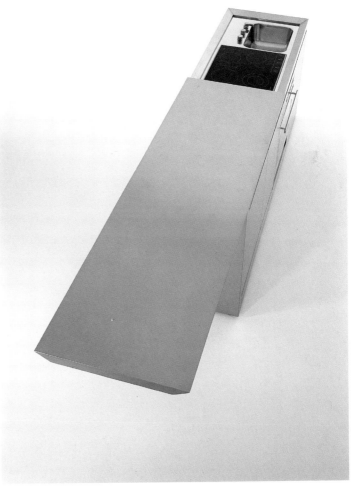

↑ →

Monoblock kitchen by Norbert Wangen for Boffi. Compact unit features sliding top, which can be used as a dining table or an extra preparation area. Stainless steel with wood finishes. Three sizes available. (H) 960 x
(L) 1590–2340 x
(D) 700mm
(38 x 63–92½ x 27½in). www.boffi.com

→

MG5 free-standing dishwasher by Baumatic. Available in red, yellow and orange. (H) 850 x (W) 600 x (D) 600mm (33½ x 23½ x 23½in). www.baumatic.com

↓

Precision 3D by Amana. Three-door fridge-freezer with separate temperature zones and full-width sliding door freezer. Stainless steel and other finishes available. (H) 1780 x (W) 915 x (D) 669mm (70 x 36 x 26½in). www.amana.com

↑

MegaChef 2 by Baumatic. Part of the Studio Solari range. Multi-language LED display. Stainless steel with mark-resistant coating. (H) 596 x (W) 596 x (D) 555mm (23½ x 23½ x 22in). www.baumatic.com

←

Precision wine cabinet by Amana. Provides three individually controlled cooling zones. Stainless steel, beech, glass. (H) 1880 x (W) 685 x (D) 650mm (74 x 27 x 26in). www.amana.com

→

Samba SB6 by Baumatic. Part of the Dance Partners range. Stainless steel. Also available in red and orange. (H) 1513 x (W) 550 x (D) 580mm (60 x 22 x 23in). www.baumatic.com

↑

BT63 built-in oven by Soo-hyun Lee and Jeon Chanyoung Lee for Samsung. Digital display panel tilts back 5 degrees for easy readability. Stainless steel, glass. www.samsung.com

←

MG1 built-in oven by Baumatic, from the Dance Partners range. Flush fitting with push-in controls creates a streamlined profile. Stainless steel. Available in vibrant red, orange or yellow. (H) 596 x (W) 596 x (D) 560mm (23½ x 23½ x 22½in). www.baumatic.com

→

Case System 2.3 by Piero Lissoni for Boffi. Modular system of base and tall units with side panels in stainless steel, Corian or wood. Stainless-steel worktop rests on a light aluminium frame, creating a void between base and top. Carcass in ivory, anthracite grey or graphite-grey melamine. Doors also available in wood veneer, Setasil or M+ in the Boffi range of colours.
www.boffi.com

↓

Artematica Multiline Titanium kitchen by Gabriele Centazzo for Valcucine. Technically advanced titanium laminate finish with aluminium frame. Various types of panels available including layered HPL in many different colours, wood-laminate, lacquered MDF and glass. Available in various configurations and dimensions.
www.valcucine.it

←

Sinetika kitchen by Arrital Cucine. Dark oak with glossy white PVC doors, unicolour white worktop and units. Available in a range of materials and finishes.
www.arritalcucine.com

↑ →

Artematica Vitrum kitchen by Valcucine. Worktop in toughened glass. Glass components can be matt or gloss, coloured or etched. Aluminium, glass, stainless steel and wood.
www.valcucine.it

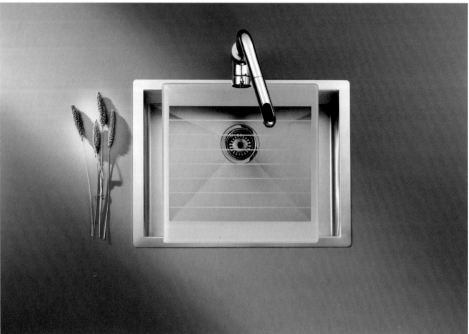

↑
Outline kitchen by Domenico Paolucci for Pedini. Features flush sinks and hobs and integral lighting. Lacquered wood, glass, aluminium and crystal worktops. A variety of other finishes and colours is also available. www.pedini.it

←
X-Tra sink by Roca. Co-ordinated glass top makes use of space over sink, providing an extra worksurface as required. Stainless steel. Available in a variety of sizes and styles. www.roca.es

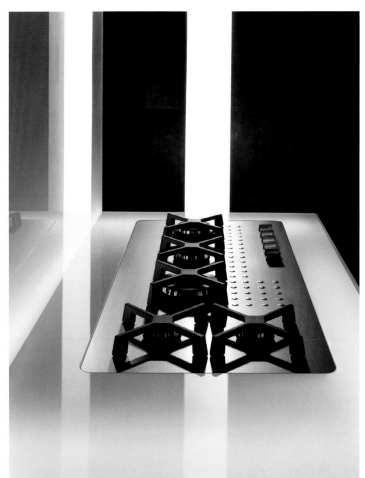

←

Jolly Nox gas hob by Barazza. Available in a wide range of shapes, configurations and burner options. Stainless steel, cast iron.
www.barazzasrl.it

↓

PVA750 Hob by Smeg. From the Linear Series of appliances. Five-burner ultra low-profile hob with a finger-friendly graphite glass base and removable cast-iron pan stands. Automatic ignition and safety valves. (W) 740 x (D) 510 x (H) 60mm (29 x 20 x 2½in).
www.smeguk.com

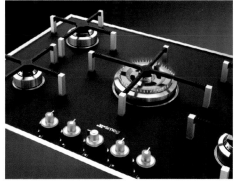

←

Matrix Varenna kitchen by Paulo Piva for Poliform. Modular design available in a variety of materials including wenge, stainless steel, glossy lacquer, glass, Corian and ebony.
www.poliform.it

→

Quadra kitchen by Arrital Cucine. Teak and glossy orange lacquered doors, worktop in Nero-sepia quartz, teak-veneered tabletop and hoods. Available in a range of materials and finishes.
www.arritalcucine.com

↑

90CM Step cooktop, part of a new built-in range by KitchenAid. Chrome frame (H) 955 x (W) 860 x (D) 510mm (37½ x 34 x 20in).
www.kitchenaid.com
www.whirlpool.com

→

Steam-Assist double oven by KitchenAid. Steam/convection oven for delicate and healthy cooking. Choose pure steam using the steam accessory, or combine it with the conventional heating elements for superheated steam. Stainless steel finish (H) 1270 x (W) 724 x (D) 660mm (50 x 28½ x 26in).
www.kitchenaid.com

Bottom Mount Fridge
and wine cooler by
KitchenAid. Available in
several configurations,
dimensions and capacities.
EasyClean stainless steel.
(H) 1805 x (W) 909 x
(D) 760mm
(71 x 35½ x 30in).
www.kitchenaid.com

Shock Freezer by
KitchenAid. Chills from
90ºC (194ºF) to 3ºC
(37.5ºF) in 90 minutes.
Shock freezing takes
food from 90ºC (194ºF)
to −18ºC (−4ºF) in 240
minutes. EasyClean steel.
(H) 595 x (W) 595 x
(D) 578mm
(23½ x 23½ x 22½in).
www.kitchenaid.com

Solitaire 11 kitchen
island by Blanco. From
the Steelart kitchen
range. Made entirely
of stainless steel with
hand-finished sinks.
www.blanco.co.uk

← K14 kitchen by Norbert Wangen for Boffi. Carcass melamine-coated, graphite-grey oak with front trim in aluminium. Plinths in stainless-steel coated aluminium. Doors finished in lacquered wood veneer. Worktops in stone, stainless steel or Corian. www.boffi.com

↑
Inspiro oven by Electrolux. Automatically selects the right temperature based on the contents of the oven, consistently achieving desired result. Rather than using a thermostat, Inspiro uses sensors to calculate energy consumption and time needed to bring food to correct temperature. When the cooking sequence is finished, the oven stops and alerts the chef that the food is ready. Stainless steel. (H) 594 x (W) 594 x (D) 567mm (23½ x 23½ x 22in). www.electrolux.com

→
Mini Om hood by Lorenzo Lispi for Elica. Tempered glass and steel. Available in a wide range of colours including black, white, electric blue, apple green and curry yellow. (H) 500–925 x (W) 550 x (D) 332mm (20–36½ x 22 x 13½in). www.elica.it

→

Wave by Fabrizio Crisa for the Evolution system by Elica. Stainless-steel cooker hood with remote control providing air purification and lighting. (H) 360 x (W) x 510 x (D) 510mm (14½ x 20 x 20in). www.elica.it

↓

Cube light hood by Team Elica. Stainless steel and tempered glass. (H) 320 x (W) 900 x (D) 360mm (13 x 35½ x 14½in). www.elica.it

←

Futura hood by David Lewis for Elica. Incorporates shelf space and halogen lighting. Tempered glass, stainless steel and aluminium. (H) 790–1030 x (W) 1198 x (D) 388mm (31½–41 x 47½ x 15½in). www.elica.it

← **Tao** by Barazza. Flush and built-in arched hob and sink. Stainless-steel shell with stainless-steel hob and sink, cast-iron pan supports.
www.barazzasrl.it

↓ **Platinum** cooker hood by Elica. Glossy stainless steel, remote control. (H) 360 x (W) 510 x (D) 510mm (14½ x 20 x 20in).
www.elica.it

↓

Chrome island chimney
hood by Elica. Halogen
lamps, stainless steel.
(H) 823–1183 x
(W) 460 x (D) 460mm
(32½–47 x 18½ x 18½in).
www.elica.it

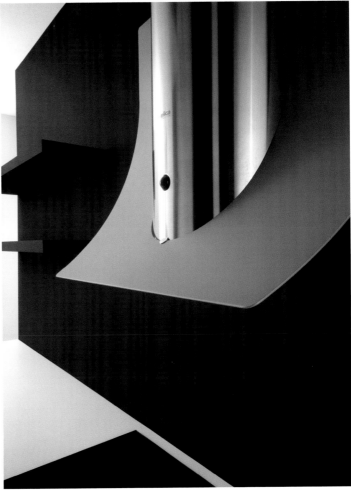

←

Elica Isolabella island
hood by Elica. Ceiling
mounted in stainless steel
and glass. Three-speed
illuminated touch sensor
with remote control.
(H) 305 x (W) 900 x
(D) 600mm (12 x
35½ x 24in).
www.elica.it

↑

Concave cooker hood
by David Lewis for Elica.
Stainless steel and
anodized aluminium,
halogen lights.
(H) 850–1250 x
(W) 898mm
(33½–49½ x 35in).
www.elica.it

Chapter five

BATHROOMS

→

Robin Levien

Robin Levien has designed bathrooms for Ideal Standard, one of the UK's leading bathroom manufacturers and the world's biggest producer of ceramic bathroom ware, for more than twenty-five years. Studio Levien now designs 20 per cent of all UK bathroom suites, but Levien's work with ceramics is not limited to bathrooms; he also designs accessories and tableware for Rosenthal, Guzzini and Villeroy & Boch.

Levien's training as a ceramist at the Royal College of Art in London has had a major influence on his career. He began work with Ideal Standard after graduating. 'I was able to translate my understanding of craft-based ceramics to the larger scale of bathroom ceramics,' he explains. 'And this skill has sustained me ever since. A friend of mine in the industry once described bathroom design as the sculpture business; this may be a less accurate description than it used to be, but it's still true that a bathroom designer's work often resembles sculpture – Ross Lovegrove's work for Vitra, for example.' Even though they are sculpting blue foam rather than marble at Studio Levien's workshop, the technique is little different from that used in the sixteenth century by Michelangelo. 'We're removing material; we can't put it back, so it's a process of form-making – it's sculpture and that's my interest in it,' says Levien. 'I know that what we do has benefited from my experience in craft and ceramics.'

Levien is also fascinated by cultural attitudes to bathrooms. 'We British don't talk much about bathroom design. Nor is the bathroom a fast-changing part of the home. I enjoy working within that historical context,' he says. 'The toilet, for example, was invented about 150 years ago and hasn't changed fundamentally since. It's made of the same material. This reflects a deep-rooted conservatism and attachment to familiar things – and that's what I enjoy being involved in.' He believes that the economy has a massive influence on design. 'When the economic climate is good, we become confident and brave and we're happy to accept the new. When it's bad, we're more cautious and traditional in our inclinations. In the past twenty or thirty years, central heating has totally transformed the way we use the bathroom in Britain. We want to spend more time in it – it's less of a practical place and more a haven for relaxation. We don't rush in and out as we used to.'

The average British bathroom is the size of a king-size bed. Does Levien see this changing? 'Bathrooms are staying small, possibly even getting smaller,' he says, 'but there's an increase in the number of en suite bathrooms. In fact, there are more bathrooms per home – that's one of the big changes. Blurring the boundaries between spaces in the home is another. It's happened with the kitchen and living room and it's now beginning to happen with the bedroom and the bathroom. Then there's concern about the environment, and water saving in particular; we're going to see more and more innovations directed towards addressing that concern.'

From his experience in working for a global brand, Levien finds that tastes vary from country to country. 'The differences are rooted in practicality,' he says. 'Everything in an American bathroom, for example, is a bit bigger, and people will pay as much for a toilet as they would for a small car. Fixtures are heavier and clunkier, more "belt and braces". The Italians are ahead of the game in terms of style, but I think that goes back to the Romans, who pretty well invented the modern bathroom – so they've been at it a lot longer than the rest of us. The amount of plumbing you can see at the back of a typical British toilet would be unacceptable in Italy at any level of the market. The Germans have some curious preferences in bathroom design, including something called a "washout toilet", which is a shelf within the toilet bowl. These differences emanate from practical issues, but they lead to aesthetic differences. The British are seen as odd because we still mainly use hot and cold taps rather than mixer taps – a hangover from old water regulations. Pillar taps make up half the sales of taps in the UK, while on the Continent and in America mixer taps are the norm.'

Designers must also take account of demographics and the ageing population. Levien is currently working on a prototype bath for elderly people – an elegant design with a removable seat and back that can be used as required. 'At the moment, this part of the market is dominated by specialist companies making horrible hoists, but we will see more and more attention paid to the fifty-plus generation who want luxury and indulgence, and why not?'

Future-proofing (creating enduring designs that don't become obsolete with age) is an increasing preoccupation for Levien. 'If you look at the bathroom now, it's kind of a disaster,' he says. 'I shouldn't really say that because I've been working on bathrooms for twenty-five years. One of the things that really bugs me is mastic – there's about two kilos of it in the average bathroom. The bathroom is made of different components that come from different places made by different companies; these parts arrive at different times and are installed by different people. And the only way to make it all work is to squidge mastic into the gaps. It's not very clever. Future bathroom design should focus on a holistic approach and come up with a way to design the room as one piece of work. Japan has led the way in this respect. The wet-room concept is an important step towards that kind of solution. The future is seamless.'

←

Spoon XL by Benedini Associates for Agape (see page 256).

↓

e-mood bathroom cabinet by Duravit from the e-mood collection. Three mirror doors, LED night-light with light sensor controlled by touch LEDs. Anodized aluminium and coloured wooden surface in cherry. (H) 720 x (W) 1000 x (D) 210mm (28 x 39 x 8in). www.duravit.com

↑

Borderline drop-in washbasin bowl 03 by Roberto and Ludovica Palomba for the Palomba Collection by Laufen. Available in a range of six ceramic washbasins with surfaces finished in WonderGliss. (H) 160 x (W) 450 x (L) 450mm (6½ x 18 x 18in). www.laufen.com

←

Blue Moon whirltub with bench by Duravit. Can be installed free-standing or against a wall. Acrylic inlay and wood in various colours. (H) 1400 x (W) 1400 x (D) 700mm (55 x 55 x 27½in). www.duravit.com

Borderline washbasin 01
by Roberto and Ludovica
Palomba for the Palomba
Collection by Laufen.
Available in a range of
six ceramic washbasins
with surfaces finished in
WonderGliss. (H) 155 x
(W) 500 x (L) 1600mm
(6 x 20 x 63in).
www.laufen.com

Amalfi bath by Victoria
+ Albert Baths. Free-
standing design supplied
with integral plinth. Made
from QUARRYCAST, white
volcanic limestone and
resin. (H) 625–850 x
(W) 800 x (L) 1640mm
(24½–33½ x 31½ x 65in).
www.vandabaths.com

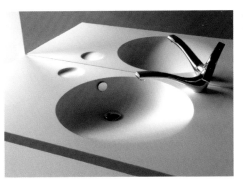

Toyo Ito washbasin and
matching tap by Toyo
Ito, from the designer's
collection for Altro. White
Corian basin available in
three sizes: (W) 700, 1150
or 1800 x (D) 550mm
(27½, 45 or 71 x 21½in).
www.altro.es

→

V140 by Samuel Heath.
Single-lever bath mixer
from the Xenon collection.
Stainless steel, chrome-
plate finish. (H) 160 x
(D) 145mm (6½ x 5½in).
www.samuel-heath.com

↓

MINIWASH by Giulio
Cappelini for Flaminia.
Wall-hung washbasin
made of Pietraluce.
Available in blue indigo,
chestnut, milky white,
anthracite, edelweiss,
white, black and sand.
Sizes: 381 x 381mm,
482 x 355mm, 254 x
406mm (15 x 15in,
19 x 14in, 10 x 16in).
www.ceramicaflaminia.it

Fontana by Giulio Cappellini for Flaminia. Made of Pietraluce, can be used as tub or deep shower tray. Black. (W) 440 x (L) 1350mm (17½ x 53in). www.ceramicaflaminia.it

↑
IO vanity basin by Alexander Duringer and Stefano Rosini, inset in bridge bench by Giulio Cappellini from the IO collection by Flaminia. Ceramic basin, wood bench, available in various sizes, colours and finishes. www.ceramicaflaminia.it

→
Rainmaker AIR overhead shower by Phoenix Design for Hansgrohe. Three all-over Whirl AIR massage jets, 350 spray outlets and five possible AIR spray modes. Integrated lighting optional. Chrome. (Diameter) 609mm (24in). www.hansgrohe.com

Raindance Rainfall showerhead by Phoenix Design for Hansgrohe. Horizontal, multifunctional shower panel with a wide water jet. Three different jet options: soft rain shower, massaging downpour and waterfall. (H of bracket) 160 x (W) 280 x (L) 548 x (D of head) 27mm (6 x 11 x 21½ x 1in). www.hansgrohe.com

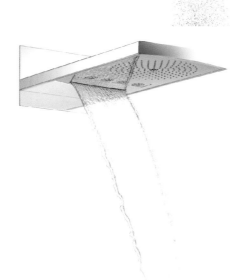

BetteFloor by Bette. Shower with flush-to-floor installation system. Steel and enamel, available in eight sizes, in white or dark grey. www.bette.de

Technoslide shower enclosure by Cesana. Aluminium frame, 8mm (½in) glass. Available in three configurations. Made to measure. www.cesana.it

←

Axor Massaud
free-standing single-lever bath or shower mixer by Jean-marie Massaud for Axor. For mounting onto bathroom floor. Hand shower, shower hose and diverter. (H) 847 x (W) 264 x (D) 380mm (33½ x 10½ x 15in). www.axor-design.com

→

Jean Nouvel thermostatic shower column by Jado. Digital program regulates temperature and water flow. Polished chrome. (H) 1122 x (W) 103 x (D) 271mm (44 x 4 x 10½in). www.jado.com

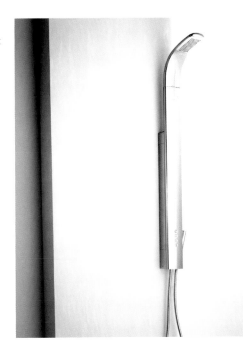

←

Jean Nouvel electronic lavatory tap with waterfall effect by Jado. Polished chrome. (W) 44 x (L) 151mm (2 x 6in). www.jado.com

← **Tris** by Ideal Standard. Shower, steam room and sauna in the space of a bathtub. Available in a variety of wood finishes. (H) 2290 x (W) 1700 x (D) 700mm (90 x 67 x 27½in). www.ideal-standard.co.uk

→ **Jean Nouvel** electronic two-hole bath/shower mixer by Jado. Digital system; water tap has no levers or handles. Polished chrome. (Projection) 201mm (8in). www.jado.com

← **Axor Citterio M** by Antonio Citterio for Axor. Single-lever basin mixer. Polished chrome. (H) 211 x (Diameter) 34mm (8 x 1½in). www.axor-design.com

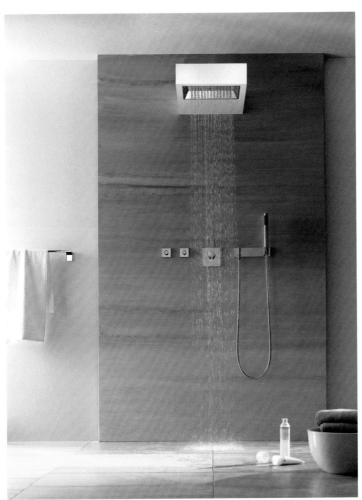

←

Sangha by Sieger Design for Dornbracht. Shower from the Elemental Spa system. Polished chrome and white Corian.
www.dornbracht.de

↓

OZ 218/1 CR bathroom and kitchen tap series by Nilo Gioacchini by Teknobili. Stainless steel. Single-hole basin mixer with anti-limestone aerator. Chrome or matt chrome. (H) 180 x (D) 110mm (7 x 4½in).
www.teknobili.it

←

Moments bathroom collection by Artefakt Studio for Ideal Standard. Comprises wall-hung drawer, storage unit, floor standing bidet, WC, basin, and bathtub with pull-out drawer. Panels available in gloss white or light oak. Rectangular bath: (W) 900 x (L) 1800mm (35½ x 71in).
www.idealstandard.co.uk

→

SingleBath bathroom collection by Hoesch. Combines many elements including futuristic mirror TV cabinet. White porcelain with walnut or macassar veneer. www.hoesch.de

↑

Hansgrohe 8in Axor Starck X Lav mixer tap by Philippe Starck for Axor. Chrome. Height of spout: 190mm (7½in). Height from mount to top of handle: 280mm (11in). Tap head depth: 150mm (6in). www.axor-design.com

→

IAM wall-mounted single-lever basin mixer with housing by Sieger Design for Dornbracht. Polished chrome and white Corian. (Projection) 185mm (7in). www.dornbracht.de

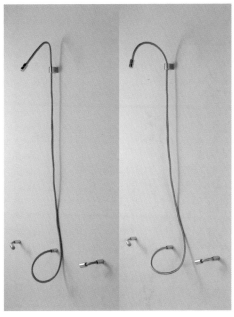

↑
Quad washbasin by Jeffrey Burnett for Boffi. White Ekotek with aluminium structure. (H) 360 x (L) 800 x (D) 220mm (14 x 31½ x 8½in). www.boffi.it

↑
NITO Sistema Sirbiss shower by Marcello Ziliani for Nito Arredamenti for Rapsel Group. Chromed brass and stainless steel. (L) 2000mm (79in). www.rapsel.it

←
Istanbul by Ross Lovegrove for VitrA. Basin mixer with pop-up. Silver. (H) 108 x (L) 181mm (4½ x 7in). www.uk.vitra.com.tr

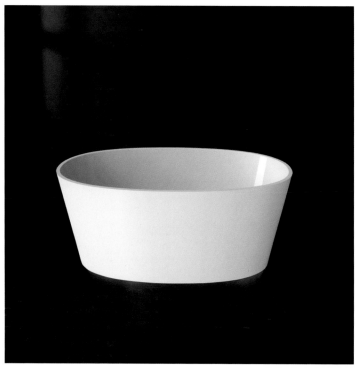

← **ios bath** by Victoria + Albert Baths. Dual-end free-standing design with integral plinth. Made from QUARRYCAST, white volcanic limestone and resin. (H) 600 x (W) 800 x (L) 1500mm (23½ x 31½ x 59in). www.vandabaths.com

↑ **T45** by MGS Progetti. Thermostatic shower and bath mixer. Part of the T45 bathroom range, which includes a variety of taps. Available in polished or satin finish. Solid stainless steel. (H) 1710 x (D) 287mm (67 x 11in). www.mgsprogetti.com

→ **Istanbul** by Ross Lovegrove for VitrA. Wall-hung washbasin. Available in four neutral colours. (H) 145 x (W) 605 x (D) 615mm (6 x 23½ x 24in). www.vitra-bathrooms.com

←

Bathtub by Matteo Thun from the Water Jewels collection for VitrA. White acrylic. (W) 750 x (L) 1700 or (W) 800 x (L) 1800mm (67 x 29½ or 71 x 31½in). www.vitra-bathrooms.com

↓

Onlyone by Lorenzo Damiani for IB Rubinetterie. Bathroom tap with flexible design that can be adjusted by manoeuvring the main body. (H) 329 x (W) 40 x (D) 105mm (13 x 1½ x 4in). www.ibrubinetterie.it

→

Cork washbasin by Alzira Peixoto and Carlos Mendonça for SimpleFormsDesign. Made of agglomerated cork and rubber-cork composite in a choice of natural colours. 380 x 140mm (15 x 5½in). www.simpleforms design.com

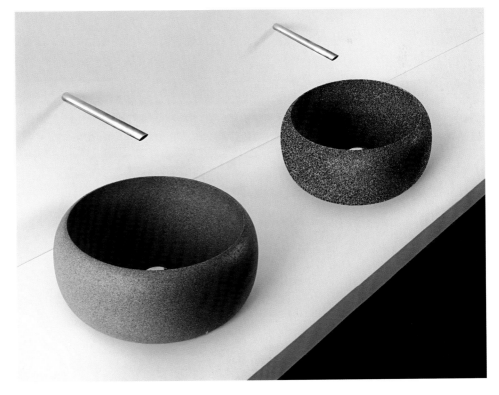

↑

MOD by Ross Lovegrove
for VitrA. Wall-hung
washbasin in white.
(H) 120 x (W) 600 x
(D) 455mm
(5 x 23½ x 18in).
www.vitra-bathrooms.com

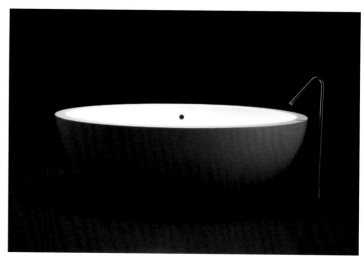

↑

Po bath by Claudio
Silvestrin for the I Fiumi
collection by Boffi. Corian
or Biheara stone. (H) 550 x
(W) x 1900 x (D) 1250mm
(22 x 75 x 49in).
www.boffi.it

←

Chiocciola shower
enclosure by Benedini
Associati for Agape.
Suitable for free-standing,
corner or recessed
locations. Shower tray
in white Exmar. Screen
wall in transparent and
translucent Parapan.
(H) 2025 x (W) 1623mm
(80 x 64in).
www.agapedesign.it

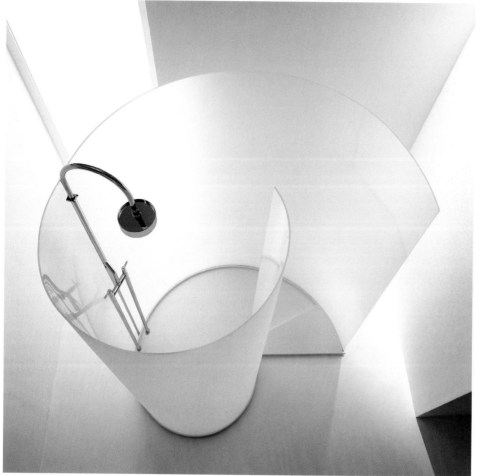

←

BK10 by Vola. Single-handle mixer with double spout and single-handle hand shower with 2m (6ft) extendable hose. Available in solid stainless steel, polished or brushed chrome and fourteen colours. (H) 464 x (W) 138mm (18 x 5½in). www.vola.dk

→

Vola HV1 Light Green by Arne Jacobsen for Vola. Available in solid stainless steel, polished or brushed chrome and fourteen colours. (H) 120 x (D) 114mm (5 x 4½in). www.vola.dk

→

Istanbul bath or shower mixer by Ross Lovegrove for VitrA. Silver. (H) 62 x spout length 225mm (2½ x 9in). www.uk.vitra.com.tr

→

INSIDE tub designed by Fabrizio Batoni for Gruppo Treesse. Ellipse-shaped design equipped with hidden waterfall tap and soft cushions. Accessories include hydromassage, chromotherapy eight-air jet system and MP3 player. (H) 700 x (W) 1900 x (L) 2350mm (27½ x 75 x 92½in). www.gruppotres.it

↑

FS1 floor-mounted bath mixer by Vola. Available in solid stainless steel, polished or brushed chrome and fourteen colours. Stainless steel, ceramic. (H) 1080mm (42½in). www.vola.dk

→

Lady-X by Giovanni Ranzoni, Luisa Frigeria and Fabrizio Proserpio for Axolo. Bathtub from the Luxury bathroom collection. Built-in thermo-insulation foam and aluminium panels. Polished satin stainless steel, wood and aluminium sheets. (H) 580 x (W) 700 x (L) 1700mm (23 x 27½ x 67in). www.axolo.it

←

050A showerhead by Vola. Can be ceiling- or wall-mounted. Available in solid stainless steel, polished or brushed chrome and fourteen colours. Polished chromed brass. (H) 50 x (W) 250 x (L) 540mm (2 x 10 x 21in). www.vola.dk

↓

Live by Mariner Concept. Double vanity unit available in eighteen colours. Stainless steel. (H) 855 x (W) 1340mm (33½ x 53in). www.mariner.it

→

Degree Shower Box 130° by bmood. Wall-shower box from the Degree collection. White tray, panels in yellow/ blue methacrylate or transparent glass. (H) 2050 x (W) 1000mm (81 x 39in). www.bmood.it

→

Malle Des Indes vanity by Decotec. One-piece basin/worktop available in three versions: lacquered MDF, zebrano wood veneer or leather-effect melamine. Available in twenty-six colours. (H) 1340 x (W) 700 x (D) 520mm (53 x 27½ x 20½in). www.decotec.fr

↓

Pear washbasin by Patricia Urquiola from the Pear bathroom range for Agape. Grey floral decorations on white. Plain white version also available. (H) 180 x (W) 550 x (D) 490mm (7 x 21½ x 19in). www.agapedesign.it

←

Splash by Jared Della Valle for M2L. Single- or double-bowl vanities, with clear glass sinks and countertops of painted glass, piano-black lacquer or various colours. (H) 300 x (W) 2400 x (D) 580mm (12 x 94 x 23in). www.m2lcollection.com

←

Bathroom mirror with light by Flaminia. Glass and chrome. Available in a range of configurations. (W) 300 x (L) 1500mm (12 x 59in).
www.ceramicaflaminia.it

↓

EXLINE bathtub by Giampaulo Benedini for Agape. Ergonomic interior modelled as chaise longue, available as island or wall-mounted unit. White Exmar. (H) 550 x (W) 700 x (L) 1700mm (21½ x 27½ x 67in).
www.agapedesign.it

↑

Max Mad bathroom tap by TresGriferia. Orange, white, green, red and black; beech and walnut options also available. (H) 180 x (W) 155 x (L) 180mm (7 x 6 x 7in).
www.tresgriferia.com

← **PLA 2** washbasin by RCR Arquitectes for Lagares. Use of Corian allows minimal, linear water outlets that do not require plugs. Available in a variety of sizes. (H) 230 x (W) 1000 x (D) 313mm (9 x 39 x 12in). www.lagares.com

↑ **Cube Sauna** by NeoQi. Features steam, aromatherapy, chromotherapy, shower and vibromassage. Can be situated against a wall, in corner or in the centre of a room. (H) 2200 x (L) 1900 x (D) 900mm (87 x 75 x 35½in). www.neoqi.com

← **Orca** washbasin by Thomas Sandell for Rapsel. White velvet or Portuguese limestone finish. (H) 150 x (W) 648 x (D) 424mm (6 x 25½ x 16½in). www.rapsel.it

← **Evok** overflowing bath by Kohler. Features aromatherapy, chromatherapy and two spa diffusion nozzles. Cast-reinforced acrylic. (W) 800 x (L) 1800 x (D) 500mm (31½ x 71 x 19½in). www.kohler.com

↓ **Kosmic Z2** steam shower cabin by Ludovica and Roberto Palomba for Kos. Features double benches, hydromassage, Turkish bath and Idrocolore colour-changing light system. Single version also available. (H) 2224 x (W) 1290 x (D) 1290mm (87½ x 51 x 51in). www.kositalia.com

↓ **Less** modular bathroom system by Castiglia Associati for Rifra. Available in various colours, sizes and finishes with wide range of glass tops and sinks plus integrated and concealed lighting. www.rifra.com

←

WT.RX washstand
by Sieger Design for
Alape in glassed steel.
New interpretation
of a 1970s classic.
(H) 900 x (W) 440mm
(35½ x 17½in).
www.alape.com

↑

PH basin with minimal
fixed spout by Boffi.
Basin in glass; spout
in stainless steel.
(H) 900 x (W) 400mm
(35½ x 15½in).
www.boffi.it

→

Betty Blue white ceramic
washstand by Alape.
(H) 850 x (W) 1200 x
(D) 600mm
(33 x 47 x 23½in).
www.alape.com

Pear bathtub by Patricia Urquiola from the Pear collection for Agape. Can be free-standing or situated against wall. Available in white or grey stone finish (illustrated). (H) 580 x (W) 930 x (L) 1840mm (23 x 36½ x 72½in). www.agapedesign.it

↑

Pear pedestal basin by Patricia Urquiola from the Pear bathroom collection for Agape. Free-standing or wall-mounted. Available in white or two-tone version (shown here) featuring a satin-finished grey exterior surface. (H) 900 x (W) 555 x (D) 409mm (35½ x 22 x 16in). www.agapedesign.it

→

Technolux single-panel bath screen by Cesana. Range includes two- and three-panel folding versions. Metal frame and glass available in various finishes. (H) 1500 x (W) 800mm (59 x 31½in). www.cesana.it

← **Geo** teak basin by William Garvey. Designed to be wall-mounted but can also be surface-mounted. Natural wood. (H) 150 x (W) 500 x (D) 400mm (6 x 19½ x 16in). www.williamgarvey.co.uk

→ **Kali'-Art-Peninsula** bathtub by WS Bath Collections. Also available as island or corner unit. External coverings including wenge and brown or black leather. (W) 800 x (L) 1800 x (D) 600mm (31½ x 71 x 23½in). www.wsbath collections.com

→ **Madera Ovales M2** by WS Bath Collections. Free-standing oval bathtub. Beech, larch, mahogany and cedar. Custom designs and made to measure also available. (H) 599 x (W) 960 x (L) 2000mm (23½ x 38 x 79in). www.wsbath collections.com

↑ **Pipé** shower by Marcel Wanders for Boffi. Stainless-steel shower pipe with floor fixings and water filter. (H) 2300 x (W) 160 x (D) 490mm (90½ x 6½ x 19in). www.boffi.it

←

Geo by William Garvey. Deep single bath in teak. Standard depth; single and double versions also available. (W) 700 x (L) 1000 x (D) 750mm (27½ x 39 x 29½in). www.williamgarvey.co.uk

↓

Bouro by Souto De Moura for Rapsel. Free-standing cylindrical ivory-stone washbasin available in two sizes. Shown here: (H) 900 x (Diameter) 500mm (35½ x 19½in). www.rapsel.it

→

Woodline V bath unit by Giampaolo Benedini for Agape. Waterproof birch-ply with natural or wenge-stained oak finish. (H) 900 x (W) 700 x (L) 1700mm (35½ x 27½ x 67in). www.agapedesign.it

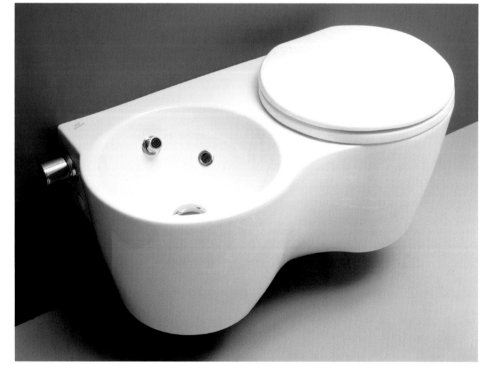

←

230710 Starck X Series
by Philippe Starck for
Duravit. Washbasin with
option of bowl on left or
right side. Ceramic with
WonderGliss surface finish
in white, platinum or
yellow. Console in chrome
or platinum. (H) 900 x
(W) 850 x (L) 1100mm
(35½ x 33 x 43in).
www.duravit.com

→

Small + T3069 by Franco
Bertoli for Ideal Standard.
Space-saving twin toilet/
bidet with seat and cover.
(H) 440 x (W) 395 x
(L) 750mm (17½ x
15½ x 29½in).
www.idealstandard.co.uk

←

Composite by Castello
Baths. Composite stone
with aluminium metallic
finish. Also available in
copper metallic finish and
full range of colours.
(H) 550 x (W) 1000 x
(L) 1780mm
(22 x 39 x 70in).
www.castellobaths.co.uk

→

Kea asymmetrical
washbasin by Marco
Piva for Rapsel. Swivel
mechanism allows it
to be rotated about
180 degrees. Basin in
Cristalplant. Shelf available
in tempered coloured
glass or wood in a variety
of finishes. Basin: (H)148 x
(W) 380 x (L) 780mm
(6 x 15 x 30½in).
www.rapsel.it

←

Freeline wooden basin by
Nico Hensel for Flowood.
Available in any colour.
(H) 85 x (W) 420 x
(L) 900mm
(3 x 16½ x 35½in).
www.flowood.de

← **Mini Soikko** bathtub from the Durat design collection. Made of DURAT, available in an extensive range of colours. Can also be tinted to cleint's specification. (H) 695 x (W) 550 x (L) 1610mm (27 x 21½ x 63in). www.durat.com

↓ **1E** washbasin by Kanera. Sculptural washbasin whose appearance is enhanced by different water levels. Available as a supported, fitted, or wall-mounted unit. Natural composite, enamelled steel. Alpine white. (H) 50 x (W) 950 x (D) 550mm (2 x 37½ x 21½in). www.kanera.de

← **Griferia tap** from the Toyo Ito collection for Altro. Stainless steel in white or chrome. (Projection) 290mm (11½in). www.altro.es

←

Porcher widespread bathroom tap, part of the Marc Newson collection for Porcher. Polished chrome. (H) 187 x (D) 117mm (7½ x 4½in). www.porcher-us.com

↓

Ellipse bath by Diamond Spas. Stainless steel/ copper. (H) 610 x (W) 1060 x (L) 1680mm (24 x 42 x 66in). www.diamondspas.com

→

Ice Light Column shower by Marcello Ziliani for Visentin. Available as a free-standing or wall-mounted shower column, as well as a wall-mounted showerhead. Equipped with a programmable light control system, a remote control and a chromotherapy system. Transparent polymethyl methacrylate. (H) 2250 x (W) 380mm (88½ x 15in). www.visentin.it

→

Cut tap by Rubinetterie
Treemme. Washbasin
mixer. Stainless steel,
chrome, brushed nickel,
white/black finish with
chrome details. (H) 263 x
(D) 157mm (10½ x 6in).
www.rubinetterie3m.it

↓

ANUBIS electronic tap by
Talocci Design for Valpra.
Stainless steel.
(H) 1236 x (D) 183mm
(48½ x 7in).
www.valpra.it

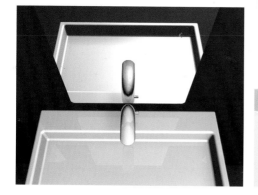

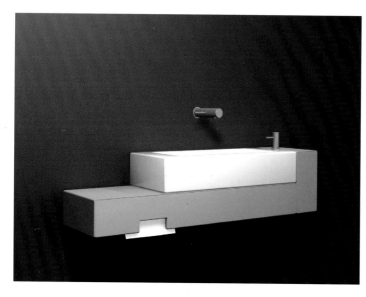

←

AquaZone by Claudia
Barkhof and Mario
Könecke for Fusioni. Series
of modular bathroom
components comprising
basins, bases and
integrated accessories.
Ceramic, MDF, painted
or veneer finish. System
available in a variety
of configurations, sizes,
finishes and colours.
www.fusioni.de

→

Nouveau wall-hung washstation by Living House. Has built-in chrome trap, washbowl and mirror with storage cabinet behind. Fibreglass body with Icetek resin basin. Shown in black; available in a variety of colours.
(H) 1224 x (W) 600 x
(D) 465mm
(48 x 23½ x 18in).
www.livinghouse.co.uk

←

Marc Newson free-standing acrylic bathtub by Ideal Standard. Bath and panels are formed as one seamless piece. (L) 1900 x (W) 950 x (D) 560mm (75 x 37½ x 22in).
www.idealstandard.co.uk

↓

TOUCH ME control electronic tap by Vicario Armando. Touch-sensitive tap; when operated a blue light illuminates. Brass with stainless-steel finish.
(H) 165 x (W) 55 x
(Projection) 110mm
(6½ x 2 x 4½in).
www.vicarioarmando.com

Anthropos cabin with furniture wall by Claudio Papa for Hansgrohe. Multifunctional shower cabin with integrated bathroom furniture. The wooden storage wall cabin incorporates a heated compartment for warming bathrobes and towels. Options include steam, aromatherapy and coloured light therapy. Sanitary acrylic tray and roof, toughened safety glass walls. Wenge, bleached sessile oak or white. (H) 2250 x (W) 1000 x (D) 1400mm (88½ x 39 x 55in). www.hansgrohe.com

Cactus tap by Aldo Cibic for Ottone Meloda. Stainless steel with chrome finish. Also available as a wall-mounted fixture. (H) 255 x (W) 140 x (D) 50mm (19 x 5½ x 2in). www.ottonemeloda.com

Technostar front-glass corner wet room by Piet Billekens for the Moods collection by Cesana. Frame in glossy, extruded aluminium, clear 8mm- (½in-) thick tempered glass. Available in clear or silver polished glass. Various sizes. www.cesana.it

← STEAM CUBE steam
cabin by Villeroy & Boch.
Multifunctional cabin for
showering, luxury massage
or steam showering.
Available in three models:
quarter circle, rectangle
and square. Sliding glass
doors, acrylic shower tray.
(H) 2200 x (W) 1200 x
(D) 1025mm
(86½ x 47 x 40in).
www.villeroy-boch.com

↑ Technovation 500 wall
spout by Cifial. U-shaped
mixer incorporating
soapdish. Available in
chrome, polished or
brushed nickel. Dish
available in white, blue
and black. (W) 150 x
(Projection) 175mm
(6 x 7½in).
www.cifial.co.uk

← Seaside bathtub by
Talocci design for
Whirlpool. Features
remote-controlled
perimeter, underwater
lights, illuminated waterfall
effect. (W) 2150 x
(L) 2000mm (84½ x 79in).
www.teuco.it

→

Oval bathtub mounted on steel structure by Ulla Tuominen for Durat. DURAT and steel, light grey. (H) 710 x (W) 755 x (L) 1710mm (28 x 29½ x 67in). www.durat.com

↑

Rain Sky E by Sieger Design for Dornbracht. Electronic shower with rain curtain, head and body spray, mist projectors, coloured lights and fragrances. Polished high-grade steel, matt high-grade steel. (W) 820 x (L) 820mm (32 x 32in). www.dornbracht.com

→

Rectangular sink on steel base by Durat. Basin in DURAT with steel base. Available in any colour required. Basin: (H) 180 x (W) 600 x (D) 500mm (7 x 23½ x 19½in). Base: (H) 670 x (W) 580 x (D) 480mm (26½ x 23 x 19in). www.durat.com

←

Kuutio by Ulla Koskinen for Durat. Washbasin wall-mounted on steel brackets. DURAT and steel. Full range of colours available. (H) 500 x (W) 500 x (D) 500mm (19½ x 19½ x 19½in). www.durat.com

↓

Halfmoon walk-in shower room by Piet Billekens, part of the Moods collection by Cesana. Chromed brass and curved panel in clear 8mm- (½in)-thick double-tempered glass in clear or silver-polished. Shower enclosure: (H) 2005 x (L) 1150mm (79 x 45in). www.cesana.it

↑

Kippo washbasin in purple by Ulla Koskinen for Durat. DURAT is a solid polyester-based material, contains recycled plastics, is itself recyclable and available in many colours. (D) 170 x (Diameter) 430mm (7 x 17in). www.durat.com

→

Simplicity cascading tap and glass sink by Ennio Arosio. Part of the Simplicity collection for Santambrogio. Glass. Made to measure. www.santambrogio milano.it

↑

Spoon XL by Benedini Associates for Agape. Bathtub made from white Exmar. (H) 500 x (W) 985 x (L) 1800mm (19½ x 39 x 71in). www.agapedesign.it

→

Cube washbasin by Benedini Associates for Agape. Birch plywood. (H) 500 x (W) 400 x (D) 400mm (19½ x 16 x 16in). www.agape.it

←

Gobi bathtub by
Marcel Wanders for
the Gobi collection for
Boffi. Constructed from
CristalPlant. Can be wall-
or top-mounted. (H) 500 x
(W) 1700 or 1900 x
(D) 750 or 850mm (19½ x
67 or 75 x 29½ or 33in).
www.boffi.it

↓

Tatami shower area by
Roberto and Ludovica
Palomba for Flaminia.
Floor-level shower tray,
composed of ceramic
elements with a non-slip
surface that also serves as
a foot massage. Ceramic
in white, anthracite,
edelweiss or black.
Four sizes available.
www.ceramicaflaminia.it

↑

Wedge single washbasin
by HighTech Design
Products AG. Concrete
with a UV waterproofing
treatment to prevent
staining. Available in dark
grey or red. (H) 120 x
(L) 1100 x (D) 500mm
(5 x 43 x 19½in).
www.hightech-design-
products.com

→

Starck X free-standing bathtub by Philippe Starck for Duravit. Features all-round water channel with stones or wooden inserts and optional individual interplays of colour. Built-in or free-standing versions available. White. (W) 1290 x (L) 2320 x (D) 600mm (51 x 91 x 23½in). www.duravit.com

↑

Hansa2day hand shower by Hansa. Tilting showerhead with spray or cascade. Chrome, coated white or black. (L) 2340mm (92in). Showerhead diameter 160mm (6in). www.hansa.com

←

Hansaclear lux showerhead by Hansa. Illuminated showerhead with colour-changing feature. Chrome and transparent acrylic. (L) 2550mm (100in). Showerhead diameter 120mm (5in). www.hansa.com

→

Hansacolourshower
shower system by Hansa.
Water- and light-bearing
shower column with
high-capacity LEDs in soft
or light rain mode. Eight
colours with four colour
sequences. Chrome.
(H) 1098 x (D) 331mm
(43 x 13in).
www.hansa.com

↓

Hansacanyon
electronically operated
mixer tap by Hansa.
Coloured illuminated glass
disc in the spout with
red/blue colour gradient.
Chrome finish. (H) 256 x
(W) 45 x (D) 100mm
(10 x 2 x 4in).
www.hansa.com

↑

Geografia by Jean Michel
Wilmotte. Inspired by
Teuco Guzzini. A changing
ensemble in which the
products, intended for
the various ways of using
water, transform into
unusual places. The basin
turns into a lake at the
top of a hill; the shower
becomes an intriguing
waterfall; and a river cuts
across the landscape
where water flows
continuously. Duralight, a
new acrylic-based surface
material. Available in
various dimensions.
www.teuco.it

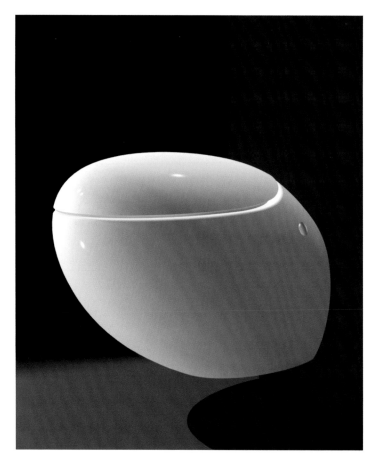

←

Alessi wall-hung WC by Stefano Giovannoni for Laufen. Removable seat and cover with soft closing hinges, white ceramic. (H) 415 x (W) 585 x (D) 390mm (16 x 23 x 15in). www.laufen.com

↓

Superplan flush-fit Lilie shower tray by Phoenix Design for Kaldewei. Steel enamel. Grey or white. Available in many different sizes. (D) 25mm (1in). Ideal for installing flush with floor. www.kaldewei.com

↑

Reverse bathtub designed by Piet Billekens for Cesana Design. Can be used as either shower or tub. Shower doors are 8mm-(½in-)thick tempered glass. White acrylic. (W) 700 x (L) 1700 up to (W) 800 x (L) 1800mm (27½ x 67 up to 31½ x 71in). www.cesana.it

← **Alessi** floor-standing washbasin by Stefano Giovannoni for Laufen. With integrated pedestal and Alessi monoblock basin mixer. White ceramic. (H) 850 x (W) 520 x (D) 530mm (33 x 20½ x 21in). www.laufen.com

↓ **Istanbul** washbasin with integrated pedestal designed by Ross Lovegrove for VitrA. Ceramic. Available in white, pergamon, orange, green, grey and beige. (H) 850 x (W) 605 x (D) 615mm (33 x 23½ x 24in). www.vitra.com.tr

→ **Argento vanity** designed by Bianchini & Capponi. Vanity unit including mirror, basin and three-piece chrome basin mixer. Reclaimed antique wood, handcrafted and painted, then silver-gilded. (H) 950 x (W) 1180 x (D) 610mm (37½ x 45½ x 23½in). Mirror (H) 920 x (W) 630mm (36 x 25in). www.bianchinicapponi.it

→

Universal bath system by Piero Lisson for Boffi. Modular system of base units with flap doors in different finishes, pull-out drawers and inner shelves in aluminium. Base units in ivory, grey or graphite grey oak. Melamine-coated. Various dimensions. www.boffi.it

↓

The Neorest, back and front 600 by TOTO. Smart loo – the lid lifts as you approach and closes as you leave. Flush is automatic. Other features include back and front flushing, drying, deodorizing and seat-warming. (H) 565 x (W) 436 x (D) 835mm (22 x 17 x 33in). www.totousa.com

↑

Scoop bathtub by Michael Schmidt for Falper. CristalPlant. (H) 480 or 550 x (L) 1690 x (D) 940mm (19 or 22 x 66½ x 37in). www.falper.it

→

Aqhayon bath by Jaime Hayon, from the AQHayon collection for Artquitect. White or black wood. Fibreglass with ceramic accessories. (H) 510 x (W) 1000 x (L) 2045mm (20 x 39 x 80½in). www.aqhayon collection.com

↑

Washbasin and stand by Jaime Hayon. Part of the AQHayon collection. for Artquitect. Ceramic and steel, laser-cut mirror. Choice of limewood, MDF, stoneware porcelain, precious metals or enamel finish. Basin available in five lacquered colours: yellow, gold, platinum, black or white. Basin stand: (H) 810 x (W) 1400mm (32 x 55in). www.aqhayon collection.com

→

Loop by usTogether bathroom. This entire range can be customized with graphics of your choice. Consists of free-standing bath, wall-mounted basin and storage unit in acrylic stone material. www.ustogether.eu

→

83 Line range by usTogether. Bathroom in acrylic stone. Consists of free-standing bath, wall-mounted basin and mirror unit. The sink and bath both contain light features with a range of colour options.
www.ustogether.eu

↑

26in sink, part of the MOD series by Ross Lovegrove for VitrA. Pedestal sink in ceramic with shelf in steel and contrasting high-gloss green. Also comes in wall-mounted version. (H) 685 x (W) 650 x (D) 455mm (27 x 25½ x 18in).
www.uk.vitra.com.tr

→

Julien soaking tub by Troy Adams for Julien. Stainless-steel construction.
(H) 1075 x (W) 1400 x (D) 1075mm
(42 x 55 x 42in).
www.julien.ca

Saphyr free-standing bathtub by Neptune. Hydrotherapy tub incorporating audio technology, turning entire acrylic shell into a speaker. Available in white, biscuit, bone or silver. (H) 571 x (W) 965 x (L) 1828mm (22½ x 38 x 72in). www.neptuneb.com

WoodIdea teak bath by Antonio Bullo for Franco Ceccotti. (H) 670 x (W) 850 x (L) 1900mm (26 x 33 x 75in). www.francoeccotti.it /www. palazzanirubinetterie.it

Ebb basin and shower unit in natural stone material by usTogether. Features overhead shower, handheld shower and basin in one sculptural unit. (H) 2200 x (W) 3750 x (D) 650mm (87 x 148 x 25½in). www.ustogether.eu

→

Escale free-standing bath
by Kohler. With integral
lumbar support. Acrylic.
Available in white, almond
and biscuit. (H) 613 x
(W) 914 x (L) 1829mm
(24 x 36 x 72in).
www.us.kohler.com

←

Le Acque bathroom
by Claudio Silvestrin for
Toscoquattro. Made of
a light stone with a bold
mottled pattern. The
bathroom includes the
free-standing bath, which
is carved from a solid rock.
Counters and cabinets are
made of dark wood.
www.toscoquattro.it

→

Dot by Wiel Arets for Il
Bagno Alessi. Single-lever
washbasin tap in chrome.
(H) 100 x (D) 62mm
(4 x 2½in).
www.alessi.com

→

Walk-in shower tray
by Bette. Teak deck and
virtually invisible drain.
Glass screens available
for niche and corner
installations. Acrylic and
teak. Available in two sizes:
(H) 1800 x (W) 900 or
(H) 1500 x (W) 1000mm
(71 x 35½ or 59 x 39in).
www.bette.de

↑

Pipé tap by Marcel
Wanders for Boffi. Fixed
wall-mounted shower tap
with red mixer handle.
Stainless steel with
satinized finish.
(D) 400 x (Diameter)
90mm (16 x 3½in).
www.boffi.it

→

Beleina whirpool bathtub
by Thalassor. Includes
massage jets, hydrojets
and a chromotherapy
system offering 512
colours. Acrylic. (W) 1500 x
(D) 1500mm (59 x 59in).
www.douche.fr

→

L10 washbasin by Norbert Wangen for Boffi. White Carrara marble washbasin. Also available in black Marquina marble. Hidden brackets, covered plug and smooth seamless surface. (H) 100 x (L) 1200 x (D) 500mm (4 x 47 x 19½in). www.boffi.it

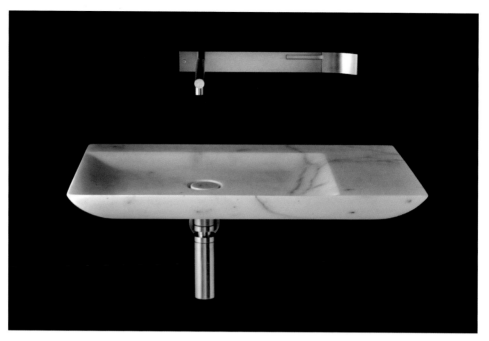

← ↑

XL showerhead by Ludovica and Roberto Palomba for Zucchetti. Stainless-steel showerhead containing 400 nozzles with rain-jet spray. Also available with central LED light. (Diameter) 500mm (19½in). www.zucchettionline.it

← **Logic Horizon** modular glass shower system by Piet Billekens for Cesana. Control panel doubles as shelf. Water flow and temperature can be adjusted from without or within. Anodized aluminium, bright finish, bar and details in chromed brass. Various dimensions. www.cesana.it

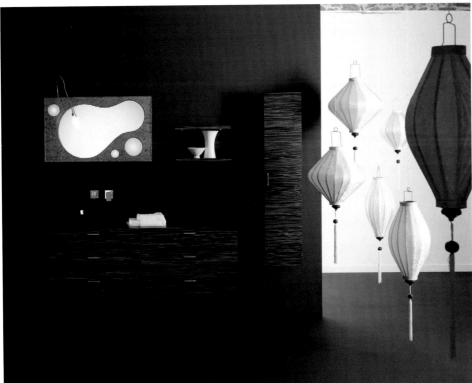

↑ **Borderline** washbasin by Ludovica and Roberto Palomba from the Palomba Collection for Laufen. Ceramic, with surface finished in WonderGliss. Available in a range of six washbasins and bowls. Range includes matching lower units (light oak or macassar ebony), mirrors and lights. (H) 135 x (W) 420 x (L) 900mm (5 x 16½ x 35½in). www.laufen.com

← **Forme** bathroom by Marco Poletti for Eurolegno. Available in different measurement and combinations of materials including ponyskin, mirrors, resins and Swarovski crystals. www.eurolegno.it

→

Modul waterfall bathroom tap by Rubinetterie Cristina. Can be wall-mounted or free-standing. Chrome, black, pink or stainless steel. (H) 210 x (W) 60 x (D) 130mm (8 x 2 x 5in). www.cristina rubinetterie.com

↓

Techno M10 tap by Cifial. Wall-mounted bath/ shower mixer makes use of the spout as the diverter, which folds tidily away when the shower is used. Chrome. (H) 200 x (W) 46 x (D) 146mm (8 x 1½ x 6in). www.cifial.co.uk

↑

Iguazu by Cristalquattro. Rectangular shower tray with non-slip glass slats, polished steel frame and drain. Various designs and dimensions. www.cristalquattro.it.

↑

WOSH tap by William Sawaya for Zucchetti. Bath/shower mixer with hand-shower set in silver stainless steel. (H) 115 x (W) 317 x (D) 215mm (4½ x 12½ x 8in). www.zucchettionline.it

↓

Sharp free-standing washbasin by Sandro Meneghello and Marco Paolelli for Artceram. Icetek. (H) 850 x (W) 500 x (D) 500mm (33 x 19½ x 19½in). www.artceram.it

↓

Moab AIS sink by Moab80. Tapless sink in white Corian. Other colours available on request. (H) 180 x (W) 1000 x (D) 540mm (7 x 39 x 21½in). www.moab80.it

←

Miss free-standing washbasin by Sandro Meneghello and Marco Paolelli for Hidra. Icetek. (H) 890 x (W) 500 x (D) 550mm (35 x 19½ x 22in). www.hidra.it

→

La Ciotola basins by Sandro Meneghello and Marco Paolelli for Artceram. Basins with coloured rims available in black, red, yellow or pink ceramic. (Diameter) 460mm (18in). www.artceram.it

↓

Rotator basin by Ron Arad for Teuco. The slowly rotating basin transforms into a shower and the continuously flowing water becomes an essential component of the design. Duralight. (Diameter) 240mm (9½in). www.teuco.it

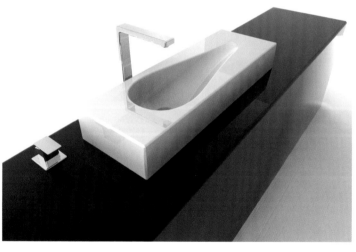

↑

Spoon basin by Sandro Meneghello and Marco Paolelli for Artceram. Counter or wall-hung versions available in two sizes. Ceramic. (W) 600 or 800 x (D) 270mm (23½ or 31½ x 11in). www.artceram.it

↓

Pitsi, lavabo, de Ulla Koskinen, para Durat. DURAT gris oscuro con motas blancas. Se fabrica en otros colores. (Altura) 500 x (anchura) 500 x (fondo) 500 mm. www.durat.com

↓

155 Degree, de BMood. Lavabo con estante movible en Cristalplant o Corian coloreado —amarillo, naranja, negro, blanco o violeta. (Altura) 450 x (diámetro) 230 mm. www.bmood.it

←

Outline, lavabo, de BMood. El lavabo de Corian y cristal parece que flota. Azul, amarillo o naranja. (Altura) 120 x (diámetro) 430 mm. www.bmood.it

→
VETRO, de Falper Design.
Consola de cristal con lavabo
ovalado de cristal integrado.
Cristal transparente y de color.
Disponible en diversos
tamaños y una amplia
gama de colores.
www.falper.it

↑
Concerto, lavabo, de Claudio
Nardi, para Toscoquattro.
El panel de cubierta de
Siltek grabado con diferentes
dibujos oculta la función.
El lavabo es de Cristalplant
blanco o negro. Disponible
en diversas estructuras
y tamaños.
www.toscoquattro.it

→
Arne, bañera ergonómica,
de Nada Nasrallah y Christian
Horner, de Soda Design,
para Rapsel. Inspirada
en los diseños de sillas de
Arne Jacobsen. Resina
de titanio. Blanca. (Altura)
940 x (anchura) 1.000 x
(longitud) 1.660 mm.
www.rapsel.it

←

Vision, lavabo con pedestal, de Nespoli E. Novara, para Rapsel. Alicrite con luz interior. (Altura) 850 x (anchura) 640 x (fondo) 490 mm.
www.rapsel.it

←

Plié, lavabo, de BMood. Perfil delgado con toallero integral. Corian blanco. (Altura) 110 x (anchura) 1.000 x (fondo) 400 mm.
www.bmood.it

↑

LIGHT, módulo con lavabo, de Falper Design. Lavabo ovalado y armario en compuesto de resina y chapado. Madera en cualquier color brillante o mate. Ocho acabados distintos. Lavabo: (altura) 170 x (anchura) 660 x (fondo) 450 mm.
www.falper.it

ILUMINACIÓN

→

Gregorio Spini

Gregorio Spini es el fundador de Kundalini, una de las empresas de lámparas más modernas de Italia, entre cuyos icónicos diseños se encuentran las lámparas de pie Atomium, de Hopf & Wortmann, y Sama, diseñada por él mismo. Spini es, a la vez, diseñador y empresario, y ha contratado a una serie de arquitectos y diseñadores para crear lámparas y muebles originales. La palabra *Kundalini* refleja el enfoque filosófico de la obra de Spini, pues este término deriva de un tipo de yoga en el que la teoría y la práctica del crecimiento espiritual se basan en el lenguaje corporal y en la meditación. «Muchas de las cuestiones que me preocupan se pueden investigar y expresar mediante la iluminación», explica Spini. «Ante todo, la iluminación es visual y puede mejorar la contemplación. Yo siempre he hablado de formas de luz más estáticas que estéticas. Pero, para mí, lo más importante es la creencia frente a la iluminación, algo que ha sido diseñado, forma nuestra percepción del mundo, y, en última instancia, de la vida misma.» Spini describe el diseño «extrasensorial», un término que ha acuñado para expresar el enfoque místico en su trabajo.

Gregorio Spini fundó Kundalini en Milán en 1996, al comienzo de una época que sería testigo de un gran auge internacional del diseño contemporáneo. «Afortunadamente, me encontré en la cima de todo ello, junto a las mejores marcas tradicionales de iluminación italianas que estaban en proceso de renovación.»

Spini ha contratado a algunos de los principales arquitectos y diseñadores del mundo, entre ellos Marzio Rusconi Clerici, Karim Rashid, Hopf & Wortmann, Giorgio Gurioli, Norman Foster y Zaha Hadid. El último proyecto de la compañía es el Abyss Spot de Osko + Deichmann, una lámpara de techo con brazos fáciles de manejar que recuerdan a las vértebras de la columna. Kundalini, recientemente, ha adquirido la famosa empresa italiana de iluminación Tronconi y ha fomentado la producción de su línea Light, la primera lámpara de mesa que utiliza LEDS (diodo emisor de luz, en sus siglas en inglés) de alto voltaje. «Mi interés por la iluminación procede de mi obsesión por las ideas pioneras. Siempre me esfuerzo por encontrar algo nuevo, por la inspiración que todavía tiene que llegar.»

Después de haber sido actor, mimo, filósofo, cantante de ópera, poeta y artista, a Spini no le falta material que le ayude a inspirarse. «No me gusta que me influya la moda —comenta—, aunque no siempre puedo evitarlo. Una vez que me doy cuenta de que puedo formar parte de una tendencia o una corriente, intento cambiar de dirección y buscar otra cosa. Me enorgullezco de no imitar a otros creadores. Podría decir que la arquitectura contemporánea me inspira más que cualquier otra cosa, pero también me interesan las tecnologías asequibles, la artesanía, los materiales nuevos y los viejos mezclados con fantasías y meditación.» Sin embargo, no considera que las artes contemporáneas sean una influencia clave en su obra, excepto la óptica y el arte cinético en su aplicación potencial.

En la actualidad, la importancia de una buena iluminación y su gran influencia en el estado anímico se reconoce mucho más que en el pasado. Al mismo tiempo, la iluminación es cada vez más técnica y más eficaz en términos de gasto de energía y materiales. Aunque es perfectamente posible iluminar una casa con luces ocultas, la gente sigue solicitando belleza y originalidad. El gran desarrollo moderno es, para Spini, la unión de la iluminación técnica, «cuyo objetivo es hacer que desaparezcan visualmente las fuentes de luz», y la iluminación inspiradora, que pretende exactamente lo contrario. Una importante tendencia entre arquitectos, expertos en iluminación e interioristas es utilizar cada vez más diseños orgánicos.

La iluminación también es responsable de gran parte del consumo de energía del mundo, lo que plantea la cuestión de la sostenibilidad. «Debido a que la sostenibilidad es cada vez más importante en nuestra sociedad, se ha producido un renacimiento de las fuentes de luz fluorescentes, porque ahorran energía. Como todos sabemos, dentro de poco, las bombillas incandescentes serán ilegales. Un nuevo enfoque consiste en investigar las posibilidades de la transmisión inalámbrica de la luz. Todos acabaremos sabiendo lo que es, pero todavía es muy pronto para hablar de ello.»

Para Spini, el LED representa la verdadera revolución tecnológica en la iluminación. «Es el LED lo que da forma a la actual percepción, especialmente en iluminación arquitectónica,» explica. Aunque la tecnología LED todavía tiene mucho camino que recorrer para igualar el rendimiento de otras fuentes de luz, no tardará mucho en convertirse en la fuente de luz predominante, pues su calidad y potencia no dejan de aumentar y su precio de disminuir. «En el campo de la iluminación, estamos introduciendo un LED de alto voltaje, un producto que es novedoso y que tendrá gran influencia en el futuro.»

Spini considera que la moda del minimalismo en interiorismo ya ha llegado a su fin, pero que la novedad de los elementos muy decorativos, como la reaparición de los estampados florales y el renacer del neobarroco, también está concluyendo. Empieza a surgir lo que él describe como «una especie de futurismo orgánico, encabezado por la obra y la visión de los principales arquitectos y diseñadores actuales». Para él, la arquitectura está cambiando la forma de nuestro planeta y «dirige el espíritu de nuestro tiempo». Spini ha empezado a colaborar con algunos influyentes arquitectos con el objeto de crear un movimiento común que estimule una nueva era de diseño inspirador. «El diseño en la actualidad debería fijarse en lo que la arquitectura expresa en cuanto a un posible lenguaje contemporáneo, o se perderá en el enfoque tradicionalista que se refiere a las grandes lecciones del movimiento moderno para considerar el diseño inspirador como una expresión individual ególatra e inútil. Existe un nuevo espíritu en la casa, pero todavía hay que trabajar mucho, desde el punto de vista del diseño, para ponerse al día con lo que la arquitectura nos está demostrando ahora.»

←

Bossa, lámpara del brasileño Fernando Prada (*véase* pág. 292).

→

Goccia H2, lámpara de
techo, de Andrea Branzi,
para Rotaliana. Difusor
de cristal soplado realizado
a mano, con acabado brillante
o grabado. Estructura interna
de cromo. Se fabrica en dos
tamaños: (altura) 1.900 x
(anchura) 165 o 230 mm.
www.elettricarotaliana.com

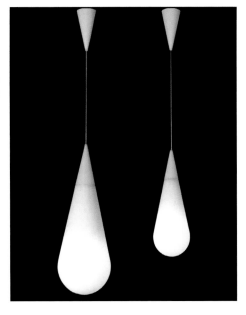

←

FARO, lámparas de mesa,
de Mindspring Lighting.
Dos dispositivos LED eficientes
dirigen un haz de luz cenital.
La base emite una luz suave
que cambia de color. Aluminio
mecanizado lacado en blanco,
negro o rojo intenso. (Altura)
310 x (anchura) 120 mm.
www.mindspringlighting.com

→

Tree Light, una de la serie
de piezas únicas diseñadas
y producidas por Front
Design. Ramas de árbol
pintadas en color rosa
fluorescente. Disponible
en diversos tamaños.
(Altura) 450-2.000 mm.
www.frontdesign.se

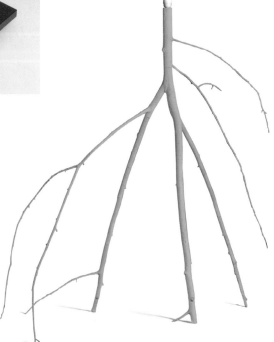

←
Porca Miseria, de Ingo
Maurer. Vajilla y cubiertos
rotos. (Altura) 1.500 x
(anchura) 1.100 mm.
www.ingo-maurer.com

←
Switch, lámpara de pie,
de Nendo, para Oluce.
Luz directa e indirecta.
Estructura y reflector de
metal, reducción de luz
mediante reflector rotatorio.
(Altura) 1.400 x (anchura)
550 x (diámetro) 400 mm.
www.oluce.com

←
Caravaggio P2, lámparas
colgantes, de Cecilie Manz,
para la serie Caravaggio
de Lightyears. Pantalla
recubierta de acero pintado
con pintura lisa negra muy
brillante. Luz directa que
no deslumbra. (Altura)
205 x (anchura) 57 mm.
Disponible en otros tamaños
y también en blanco.
www.lightyears.dk

→

Secto 4210, lámpara de pie, de Seppo Koho, de Secto Design. Pantalla de listones de madera de abedul en blanco o natural con la parte superior lacada en polvo gris. El mismo modelo se fabrica en lámparas de pared, de mesa y colgantes. (Altura) 1.750-1.850 x (diámetro) 300 mm. www.sectodesign.fi

↑

Tulip C&F, lámpara de mesa y de pie, de Seyhan Ozdemir, para Autoban De La Espada. Varillas chapadas de latón con pantalla de tela en negro o blanco. Disponible en diversas alturas: 850-1.560 x (diámetro) 400 mm. www.autoban-delaespa da.com

←

Saffron Flower, de Jonathan Coles, en colaboración con RF lighting. Se fabrica por encargo. Seis cables de fibra óptica que funcionan mediante dos dispositivos HID y que pasan del blanco al azul. (Altura) 3.500 x (diámetro) 1.400 mm. www.jonathancoles.co.uk

←

El Sphere, de Tuukka Halonen.
Cable electroluminiscente
y tubos acrílicos claros
en formas tridimensionales.
Disponible en diversos
colores. (Diámetro) 650 mm.
www.tuukkahalonen.com

↓

Swing and Jazz, LED RGB,
de Swarovski Contemporary
Lighting. Foco cuadrado
(o redondo) empotrado,
con lámparas de LED.
Marco de acero cepillado;
se puede instalar en el suelo
o en la pared; opciones
multicolores, paredes
pintadas con veladura
con efectos brillantes.
(Altura) 115 x (longitud)
115 x (fondo) 104 mm.
www.swarovski.com/
architecture

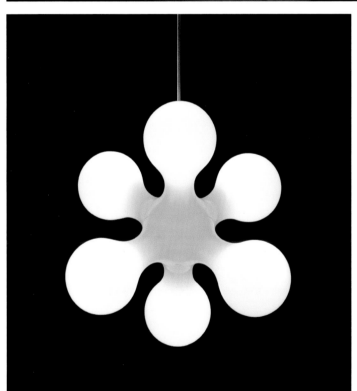

←

Atomium, lámpara colgante,
de Hopf & Wortmann,
para Kundalini. Difusor
de polietileno moldeado
por rotación que utiliza seis
fuentes de luz. También
se fabrica la versión de pie.
(Diámetro) 760 mm.
www.kundalini.it

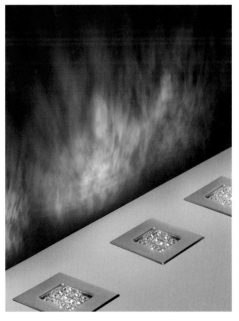

↓ →

Zucco, lámpara colgante, de Massimo Crema y Ermano Rocchi, para Melograno Blu. Cristal soplado esmerilado o transparente. (Altura) 200 x (anchura) 600 mm. www.melogranoblu.com

←

Non Random, lámparas colgantes, de Bertjan Pot, para Moooi. Pantalla de aluminio lacado al polvo, aluminio reforzado y fibra de vidrio con resina epoxi reducida. Disponible en blanco o en negro. (Altura) 700 x (diámetro) 710 mm. www.moooi.nl

←

Jolin, lámpara colgante,
de Susanne Philippson, para
Pallucco Italia. Pantallas en
tela con diminutas cuentas
de cristal que se asemejan
a la escarcha cuando se
miran desde un ángulo.
Se fabrican en negro, blanco,
gris plateado y naranja
y también en lámparas
de pie. Dos tamaños.
Pequeño: (altura) 360 x
(anchura) 620 x (diámetro)
370 mm. Grande: (altura)
430 x (anchura) 770 x
(diámetro) 480 mm.
www.pallucco.net

→

Rainy Day Light, de
Kazuhiro Yamanaka, para
Pallucco Italia. Lámpara
circular de pie o como
aplique. Fácil de trasladar
gracias al cable eléctrico
de 8 m de longitud.
Polietileno moldeado.
Blanco translúcido o
amarillo verdoso translúcido.
(Anchura)100 x diámetro
exterior 500 mm.
www.pallucco.net

LightAir IonFlow 50Sky, de Michael Malmborg, para LightAir. Lámpara colgante con purificador de bajo consumo que purifica un 99 % del aire. (Altura) 350 x (anchura) 130 mm.
www.lightair.com

↓

NOX, lámpara colgante, de Jakob Staer, de Refer and Staer. Aluminio, acero y fibra óptica. La luz proviene del «downlight» y de las fibras ópticas. (Altura) 111 x (diámetro) 650 mm.
www.refer-staer.dk

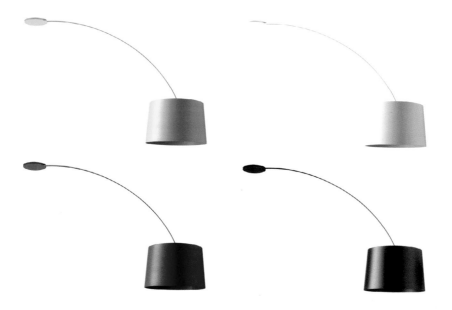

←

Twiggy Soffito, lámpara colgante, de Marc Sadler, para Foscarini. Rota 330°: una solución óptima para descentralizar la fuente de luz. Disponible en diversos colores. (Altura) 780 x (longitud) 1.700 mm.
www.foscarini.com

←

Stout Light, de Tom Dixon.
Serie de lámparas colgantes
en latón cincelado a mano
con pátina negra exterior
y dorada en el interior. Se
puede colgar una o varias
juntas con otras lámparas
de la gama Beat.
(Anchura) 520 mm.
www.tomdixon.net

←

Sheherazade, araña,
de Sophie Refer, para
la compañía danesa
Refer+Staer. Cristal soplado
artesanalmente; interior
en blanco y exterior en
negro. Veintiséis lágrimas
de cristal. (Altura) 450 x
(diámetro) 340 mm.
www.refer-staer.dk

↑

Camouflage, lámpara
colgante, de Front Design,
para Zero of Sweden.
Aluminio cortado al
láser pintado en blanco.
(Diámetro) 800 x
caída 1.500 mm.
www.zero.se

→

Leaf Light (lámpara hoja), de Yves Behar, para Herman Miller. Tiene LED ajustable con control táctil. Hojas de aluminio pulidas, pintadas o anodizadas. La hoja se extiende y se puede girar, lo que permite obtener una intensa luz ambiental. Ulitiza menos de 12 vatios. Disponible en negro, níquel o rojo. (Altura) 580 x (diámetro) 220 mm. www.hermanmiller.com

←

Campanille, lámpara colgante, de Vido Pedrals, para Diart. En negro o en cristal transparente. (Altura) 350 x (anchura) 350 x caída 1.500 mm. www.diart.es

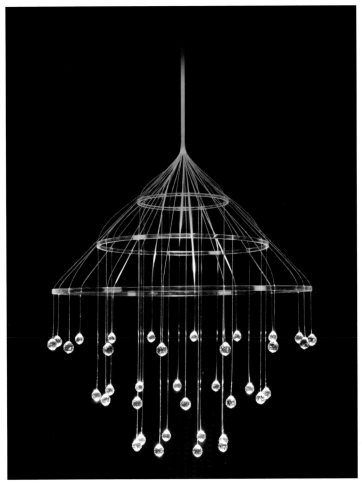

←

Scintilla 60, de Simon Breunner, para Neues Licht. Araña de fibra óptica de bajo consumo con 37 lágrimas de cristal. (Altura) 600 x (diámetro) 640 mm. También se fabrica un modelo de mayor tamaño. www.neueslicht.de

↑

VV04 V, lámpara colgante negra de Héctor Serrano, para Arturo Álvarez. Estructura metálica y policarbonato. (Altura) 1.500 x (diámetro) 800 mm. www.arturo-alvarez.com

→

Lámpara de pie Lola, de Alberto Meda y Paolo Rizzato, para Luceplan. Pie telescópico de aluminio que permite ajustar la altura. Reflector regulado por una pequeña barilla en el cabezal; produce una luz difusa y luz directa. Disponible en acabado natural o en negro. (Altura) 1.600-2.000 x diámetro de la base 480 mm. www.luceplan.it

↓

Floob, lámpara colgante, de Karim Rashid, para Kundalini. Reflector de metacrilato termoformado y extruido con aluminio centrifugado cortado al láser y difusor integrado de cristal grabado al ácido. Varios colores. (Altura) 600 x (anchura) 450 mm. www.kundalini.it

↑

Convivio, lámpara de pared o de techo, de Luta Bettonica y Mario Melocchi, para Cini & Nils. Esfera pequeña con lente de cristal óptico que proyecta un círculo de luz, mitad lente, mitad metal, con acabado cromado o en níquel satinado. (Diámetro) 110 mm. www.cinienils.com

→

Shakti, aplique con doble lámpara, de Marzio Rusconi Clerici, para Kundalini. Difusor de luz tubular en metacrilato cortado al láser. Disponible en versión para instalar directamente en la pared o con cable, enchufe y dimmer. (Altura) 800 x (diámetro) 100 mm. www.kundalini.it

← **Spiralight** by Robin Carpenter. Chandelier composed of a twisting strand of 216 LEDs suspended by a thin wire. Approximate dimensions (H) 450 x (Diameter) 1250mm (18 x 49in). www.robincarpenter.com

← **Abyss** by Osko+Deichmann for Kundalini. Table lamp made using a modular structure of injection-moulded opal polycarbonate illuminated by a high-voltage LED strip. (Diameter) 1110mm (43in). www.kundalini.it

↑ **Collage** pendant by Louise Campbell for Louis Poulsen. Constructed using three pieces of laser-cut, glossy, extruded acrylic, providing an almost endless row of combinations of patterns. Available in pink, orange, yellow, smoke-tinted or white. (H) 360 x (W) 600mm (14 x 24in). www.louispoulsen.com

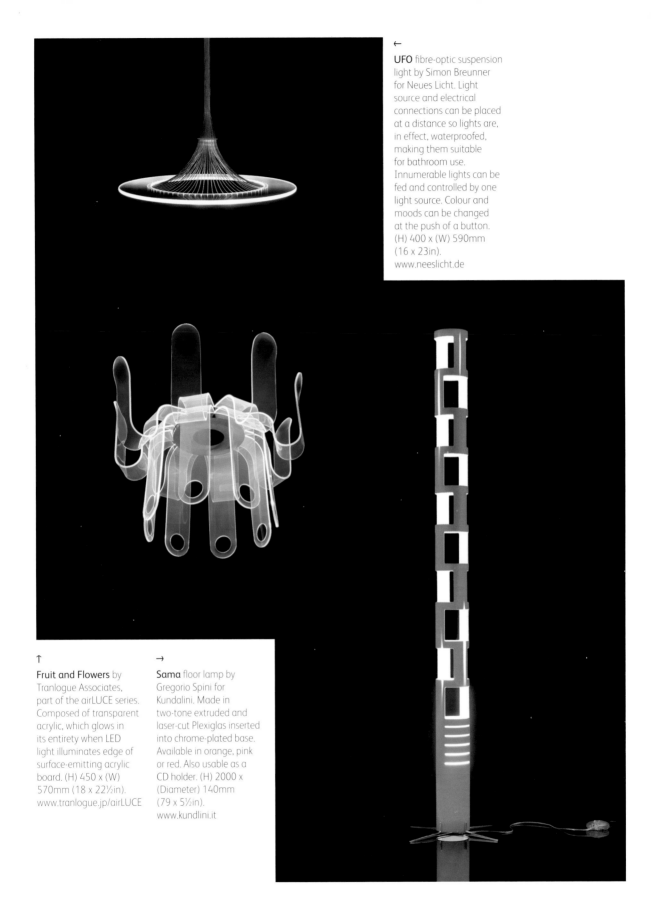

←

UFO fibre-optic suspension light by Simon Breunner for Neues Licht. Light source and electrical connections can be placed at a distance so lights are, in effect, waterproofed, making them suitable for bathroom use. Innumerable lights can be fed and controlled by one light source. Colour and moods can be changed at the push of a button. (H) 400 x (W) 590mm (16 x 23in).
www.neeslicht.de

↑

Fruit and Flowers by Tranlogue Associates, part of the airLUCE series. Composed of transparent acrylic, which glows in its entirety when LED light illuminates edge of surface-emitting acrylic board. (H) 450 x (W) 570mm (18 x 22½in).
www.tranlogue.jp/airLUCE

→

Sama floor lamp by Gregorio Spini for Kundalini. Made in two-tone extruded and laser-cut Plexiglas inserted into chrome-plated base. Available in orange, pink or red. Also usable as a CD holder. (H) 2000 x (Diameter) 140mm (79 x 5½in).
www.kundlini.it

←

Uto light by Lagranja design for Foscarini. Silicone rubber, diffuser in polycarbonate; indoor/outdoor use. Available in a choice of three colours. Flexible design for floors, walls, ceilings and more. (L) 3200 x (Diameter) 200mm (126 x 8in). www.foscarini.com

↓

Helsinki Lighthouse light installation/lamp by Timo Salli for Saas Instruments Oy. Light fibre and acrylic tube. Available in two sizes. (H) 500 x (W) 700–1200mm (19½ x 27½–47in). www.saas.fi

→

Fold floor lamp by Alexander Taylor for Established and Sons. Folded powder-coated aluminium. Signal white, damson, sulphur yellow and textured black. (H) 1550 x (W) 450mm (61 x 18in). www.establishedandsons.com

→

Dahlia lamp wall/ceiling sconce by Janne Kyttanen of Freedom of Creation (FOC) Netherlands, a company specializing in rapid prototyping. Inspired by the mathematics of nature. White laser-sintered polyamide. (Diameter) 160, 320 or 500mm (6, 12½ or 19½in). www.freedomof creation.com

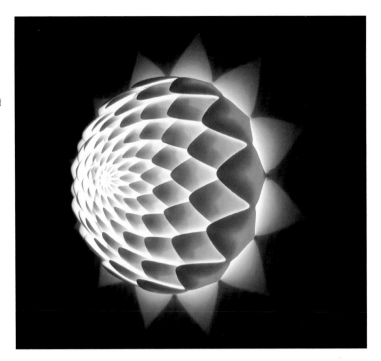

↓

Bossa pendant luminaire by Brazilian Fernando Prada. Handmade aluminium, powder-coated in matt black or white. Can be adjusted to provide direct or indirect light. (H) 300 x (Diameter) 500mm (12 x 19½in). www.lumini.com.br

↑

Agave suspension lights by Diego Rossi and Raffaele Tedessco for Luceplan. Available in three shapes. Body of lamp consists of ribs in injection-moulded transparent methacrylate, providing transparency and brightness. A set of yellow, red, green and blue filters makes it possible to change predominant colour of lamp and the light generated. Drop 1500–3000 x (Diameter) 700mm (59–118 x 27½in). www.luceplan.com

←

1597 lamp wall or ceiling sconce designed by Janne Kyttanen of Freedom of Creation (FOC) Netherlands, a company specializing in rapid prototyping. Lamp based on the Fibonacci sequence of numbers. Laser-sintered polyamide. (Diameter) 320 or 500mm (12½ or 19½in). www.freedomof creation.com

↓

Aldeberan Zig Zag Swarovski crystal chandelier by Rosita and Ottavio Missoni for the Swarovski Crystal Palace collection. Fringing consists of rows of crystals alternated with Missoni fabric, highlighted by halogen lighting within the structure. (H) 2000 x (W) 2000mm (79 x 79in). www.swarovski sparkles.com

↑

Asana sculptural chair with integral light designed by Giorgio Gurioli for Kundalini. Lacquered fibreglass on a chromed steel base. Light diffuser, hand-blown Murano glass. Available in white, black, orange and red. (H) 2050 x (W) 640mm (81 x 25in). www.kundalini.it

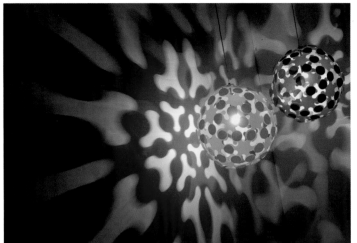

← **Hoppy** suspension light by BOO (Ben Oostrum Ontwerpt), manufactured by Belgian company Dark. Polypropylene. Design based on the mathematical principles of Buckminster Fuller's geodesic domes; consists of thirty-two faces, twenty hexagons and twelve pentagons. Approximate diameter 430mm (17in). Sold as flat pack. www.dark.be

↑ **Mini Mikado** pendant light by Miguel Herranz for Luzifer. Natural ash, stained white. Available in various colours and versions that includes table and floor lamps. (H) 570 x (W) 700mm (22½ x 27½in). www.luziferlamps.com

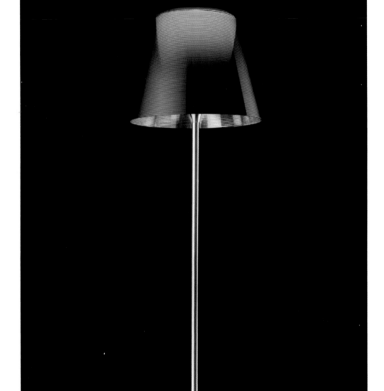

← **K floor lamp** with diffused light emissions by Philippe Starck for Flos. The K 'tribe' includes floor, table and wall lights in various sizes. Chrome-plated steel structure, outer diffuser, available in metacrylate or fabric. (H) 1830 x (W) 550mm (72 x 21½in). www.flos.com

→
Reveal by Adam Frank. Limited edition. Projector provides ambient lighting, creating the illusion of natural sunlight through a window breeze through the trees. Stainless steel, polyethylene base. Approximate dimensions of projector (H) 200 x (W) 150 x (L) 200mm (8 x 6 x 8in). www.adamfrank.com

←
Cross-Light by BOO (Ben Oostrum Ontwerpt). Pendant/table light. Wall version also available. Polyethylene. White, orange, red or green. (H) 380 x (W) 380mm (15 x 15in). www.dark.be

↑
Creepers room divider by Lionel T. Dean of Futurefactories for Materialise-mgx Belgium. Modular LED lighting system made up of stems that clip between vertical low-voltage suspension cables. SLS nylon. Individual stem length 280mm (11in). www.materialise-mgx.com

↑

Smithfield suspension
lights by Jasper Morrison.
Moulded honeycomb grid
diffuses light, avoiding
glare. Colours as shown.
Approximate dimensions:
(H) 450 x (W) 350mm
(18 x 14in).
www.architonic.com

←

Spun Light F floor lamp
by Sebastian Wrong for
Flos. Spun metal, die-cast
aluminium, polycarbonate
and sand-blasted glass.
Comes in black, brown,
grey and white, and gloss
and matt finishes. Also
available as table lamp
in two sizes. (H) 1760 x
(W) 500mm (69 x 19½in).
www.flos.com

↑

Dear Ingo by Ron Gilad
for Moooi. Powder-coated
steel suspension light
combines familiar objects
in an unexpected and
striking manner. Available
in black. (H) 800 x
(Diameter) 1000mm
(31½ x 39in).
www.moooi.com

→

Chasen suspension light by Patricia Urquiola for Flos. Fine, flexible steel strips allow fitting to be reshaped to allow more or less light to be emitted. Also available as table lamp. Colour as shown. (H) 600 x (W) 300mm (23½ x 12in). www.flos.com

→

Proper pendant lamp by Lisa Widén and Anna Irinarchos of WIS Design. Painted plywood with a net of brass. Colour as shown. (H) 270 x (W) 560mm (10½ x 22in). www.rydensgnosjo.se

→

Tab floor lamp by Barber Osgerby for Flos. Die-cast aluminium shade, extruded aluminium stand, reflector-engineered ceramic. Also available as desk and wall lamp. (H) 1700 x (W) 341mm (67 x 13½in). www.flos.com

←

Dot floor lamp by
Lisa Widén and Anna
Irinarchos of WIS Design.
Metal switch mechanism,
inspired by a pearl
necklace. Various colours.
(H) 1600 x (W) 370mm
(63 x 14½in).
www.lampister.com

↓

Empire floor lamp by Luca
Nichetto for Foscarini.
Iridescent methacrylate
diffuser and base/screen in
transparent polycarbonate.
Colours: metallic pearly
white and copper/bronze.
(H) 1900 x (W) 310 x
(D) 210mm
(75 x 12 x 8in).
www.foscarini.com

→

Orchadia illuminated
metal mobile by sculptor
Rodger Stevens and
designer Mark McKenna.
Special printed circuit-
construction technique
shapes the illumination
system, pushing low-
voltage current to
super-tiny incandescent
light sources.
www.mmckenna.com

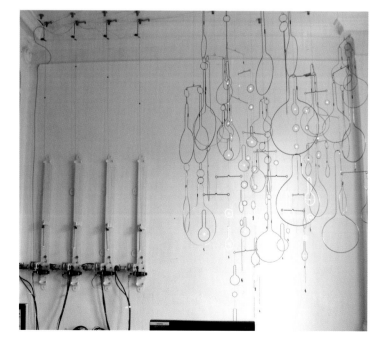

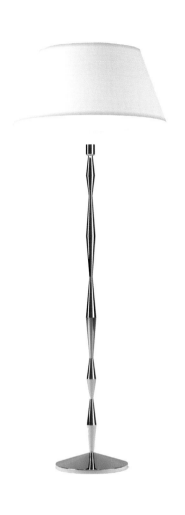

↑

Levitating lamp from the Magical collection by Front Design. Lampshade appears to levitate above invisible light source. Produced in a limited edition at Galerie Kreo, Paris. Base: (H) 1590 x (W) 370mm (62½ x 14½in). Shade: (H) 130 x (W) 680mm (5 x 27in). Total height: 2000mm (79in). www.galeriekreo.com

↑

Cage light by Tom Dixon. Wire copper-plated steel, laminated cotton shade. (H) 600 x (W) 300mm (23½ x 12in). www.tomdixon.net

←

Aretha floor lamp with reflected light by Ferruccio Laviani. Two-colour lacquered aluminium. (H) 1800 x (W) 300 x (D) 140mm (71 x 12 x 55in). www.foscarini.com

→

Fields by Vicente Garcia Jimenez for Foscarini. Modular wall light composed of methacrylic sheet and aluminium, organized in three different elements that can be installed either individually or in a combination to achieve a range of decorative effects. (H) 950 x (W) 1780 x (D) 230mm (37½ x 70 x 9in). www.foscarini.com

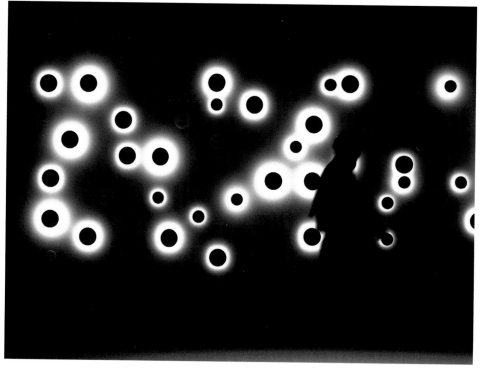

←

Kaleidolight by Ali Ganjavian to commission only. Installation of glass cylinders with aluminium lids, inserted into a wall with varying degrees of insertion/protrusion, affecting the intensity of light filtered in. www.tik-tac.com

CAO MAO white wall light by Hopf & Wortmann of Buro Fur Form. Polypropylene, white only. Available in two sizes. (H) 700 or 210 x (Diameter) 700 or 1200mm (27½ or 8 x 27½ or 47in). www.next.de

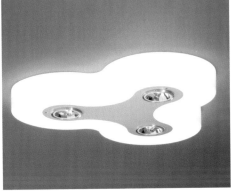

↑

Cloud ceiling light by Klaus Baulmann and Sundern-Langscheid for Schmitz-Leuchten. Anodized aluminium and white acrylic glass provides a combination of free-shining and directed light. Energy-saving fluorescent lamps with low voltage. (H) 740 x (W) 790 x (D) 80mm (29 x 31 x 3in). www.schmitz-leuchten.de

←

Tubor 9 suspension light by Lionel T. Dean of FutureFactories. Laser-sintered nylon. Example of digital manufacturing offering infinite permutations. (H) 300 x (W) 210 x (D) 200mm (12 x 8½ x 8in). www.FutureFactories.com

→

Bombay Sapphire light by Paul Cocksedge. Design involves pouring gin and tonic into a suspended lightbulb-shaped vessel lit with a UV LED. Switched on, the clear liquid glows blue and the liquid becomes the light. (Diameter) 300mm (12in). www.paulcocksedge.com

↓

Crossed wall light by Partridge & Walmsley for Benchmark Furniture. Oak, available in two sizes (small shown here). (H) 550 x (W) 610mm (21½ x 24in). www.benchmark-furniture.com

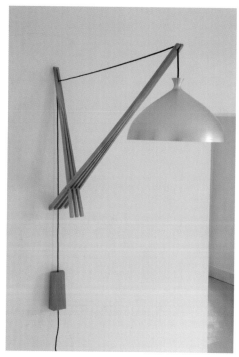

→

Leading Light floor lamp by Terence Conran for Benchmark Furniture. Walnut shelf, lacquered metal tripod legs. Shown here with drum shade in pleated silk. (H) 1670mm (66in). www.benchmark furniture.com

→ **Tail Light 2007** by Stuart Haygarth. Recycled vehicle light lenses grouped by style and size and attached to acrylic boxes to form robotic structures. Edition of seven (plus two artist's pieces). Two sizes. Fat: (H) 1420 x (W) 570mm (56 x 22½in). Slim: (H) 1520 x (W) 520mm (60 x 20½in). www.stuarthaygarth.com

↑ **Yo-Yo** pendant light by Francesco Giannattasio for Modo Luce. Plexiglas mirror, decorative external ring in satin finish, chrome detail. Suitable for bathroom use. Available in black, white or red. (Diameter) 480mm (19in). www.modoluce.com

← **Illuminated cornice** by John Harrington. Cast architectural detail in clear polyurethane resin, bead-sand-blasted to diffuse light. Supplied in lengths of 1.8m (71in); (W) 210mm (8in), complete with an attachment system. www.johnharrington.co.uk

→

Pandora kinetic chandelier by Fredrickson Stallard for Swarovski Crystal Palace collection. Constructed from 1990 crystals, the form of the chandelier is constantly destroyed and recreated through movement generated by computer-controlled servo motors. (H) 2400–4000 x (Diameter) 4000mm (94–157 x 157in). www.swarovski sparkles.com

↓

PizzaKobra extending table lamp by Ron Arad for iGuzzini. Curls neatly into a flat spiral when not in use. Steel and aluminium with chrome finish. (H) 185–773 extended x (Diameter) 260mm (7–30½ x 10in). www.iguzzini.com

←

Marrakesh by Mindspring. Modular LED lighting system composed of expandable interlocking aluminium modules. Light can be direct or reflected. Available with soft white light or RGB light. Various colours. www.mindspring-lighting.com

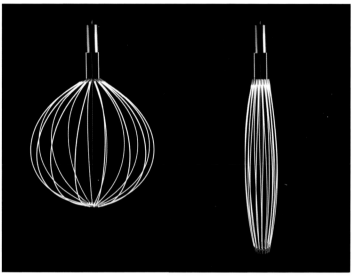

Dandelion lights by Sung Hwa Jang for p45. Shades 100 % polyester, 8mm (½in) steel stem, allows gentle movement. (H) 1240–1630 x (W) 150 x (D) 150mm (49–63 x 6 x 6in). www.sunghwajang.org

↑

Medusa by Mikko Paakkanen for Saas. Side-emitting fibre-optic rods lit by high-intensity LEDs. Microprocessor-controlled motor changes shape of fitting. Dimensions vary: (H) 1500–1900 x (W) 250–1000mm (59–75 x 10–39in). www.saas.fi

←

Optical chandelier by Stuart Haygarth. Composed of 1,020 pairs of prescription spectacles. Creates mirror-ball effect as light is refracted through layers of lenses. Edition of ten. Two sizes. Large: (L) 2300 x (Diameter) 1000mm (90½ x 39in). Small: (L) 1500 x (Diameter) 800mm (59 x 31½in). www.stuarthaygarth.com

→ **Neutra** suspension light by Ferruccio Laviani for Kartell. In PPMA (plastic). Consists of two elements similar to two shells that enclose the structure. Large-sized circular lamp, ideal for big spaces. Available in black and white. (Diameter) 900mm (35½in). www.kartell.it

↑
Guardian of Light
floor lamp by Susanne Philippson for Pallucco Italia. Painted metal stand, silkscreen-printed polycarbonate shade with trim in black, white and aluminium grey. Peels back to reveal a light lining. (H) 1800 x base diameter 500mm (71 x 19½in). www.palluccobellato.net

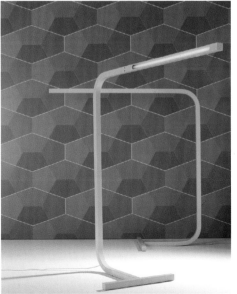

← **Angle Floor Light** by Tom Dixon. Cantilevered, directional task light made of bent extruded aluminium in off-white powder coating. Lamphead rotates through 180 degrees to provide multidirectional lighting. (H) 1400 x (W) 400mm (55 x 16in). www.tomdixon.net

→
Skygarden pendant light by Marcel Wanders for Flos. Chalk body with decorations in relief interior; liquid-painted exterior. Available in white, black, opal-gold and rust. (Diameter) 600mm (24in). www.flos.com

↑
Allegro by Atelier 01. Range of linear extruded aluminium wirelights, perfect for large spaces. Available in three shapes and chromatic finishes. Shown here from left to right: Allegro vivace, Allegro assai and Allegro ritmico. (H) 810–1360mm x (W) 640–1360mm (32–53½ x 25–53½in). www.foscarini.com

←
Deluxe 35S by Archirivolto for Murano Due. Pendant light, chromed metal, satin finish, layered blown-glass diffuser, creating continuous play of light and shade. Available in white or black. (H) 1200 x (Diameter) 500mm (47 x 19½in). www.muranodue.com

→
D-Tour floor lamp by Martino d'Esposito. Stem emphasizes switch by making a little detour around it. Stainless steel. (H) 1730 x (W) 3800mm (68 x 150in). www.neweba.com

←

Bubblicious pendant light by Chris Kabel. Hand-blown glass lampshade. Limited batch production by Iris Roskam. Various colours including white, lustre gold and lustre silver. Diameter variable from 300 to 500mm (12 to 19½in). www.chriskabel.com

↓

Booklamp by Seyhan Ozdemir and Sefer Çagler for Autoban. Available in oak or walnut with fabric shade. (H) 1380 x (W) 565 x (L) 400mm (54 x 22 x 16in). www.autoban-delae spada.com

→

Gregg table lamp by Ludocica and Robert Palomba for Foscarini. Satinized, free-blown glass. Three sizes: piccola, media and grande. Suspension, ceiling and wall versions also available. (H) 111–400 x (W) 130–470mm (4–16 x 5–18½in). www.foscarini.com

← **Dandilight** floor lamp by Benjamin Hubert. Also available as pendant. Resin-cast lamp, sand-blasted aluminium stand. (H) 1500 x (W) 500mm (59 x 19½in). www.benjamin hubert.co.uk

← **Arkipelag** floor lamp with table by Niclas Hoflin, manufactured by Ruben Lighting. Matt or glossy finishes; various colours. (H) 1600 x (Diameter) 300mm (63 x 12in). www.rubenlighting.com

← **Polyp** pendant light by Marie Moerel for Cappellini. White ceramic. (H) 530 x (W) 330 x (D) 300mm (21 x 13 x 12in). www.cappellini.it

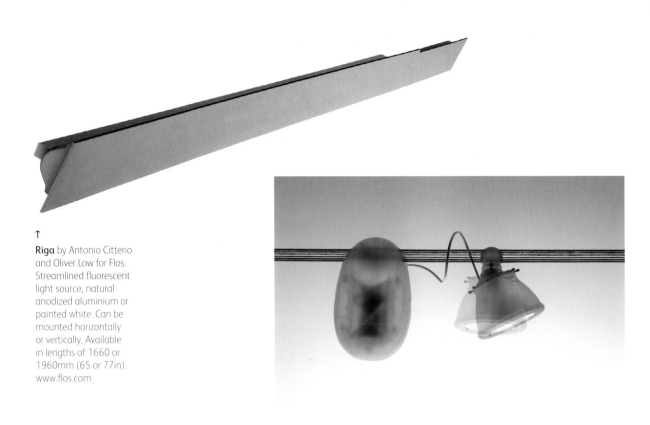

↑

Riga by Antonio Citterio and Oliver Low for Flos. Streamlined fluorescent light source, natural anodized aluminium or painted white. Can be mounted horizontally or vertically. Available in lengths of 1660 or 1960mm (65 or 77in). www.flos.com

↑

Silk cable lighting system by Tobia Scarpa for Mizar. Flexible system, ideal for difficult architectural spaces. Cable allows independent control of the three-dimensional aluminium light fittings. Light fittings (L) 145 x (Diameter) 128mm (5½ x 5in). www.mizarlighting.com

←

DOME table lamp by Todd Bracher for Mater. Steel shade in black or white. (H) 380 x (Diameter) 400mm (15 x 16in). www.materdesign.com

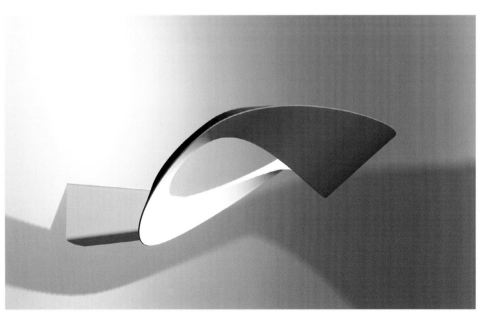

←

Nomad pendant light by Niclas Hoflin for Ruben Lighting. Black, glossy shade. Available in small, medium or large sizes. (H) 200–320 x (Diameter) 90–300mm (8–12½ x 3½–12in). www.rubenlighting.com

←

VORTEXX chandelier by Zaha Hadid and Patrik Schumacher. Manufactured by Zumtobel in collaboration with SAWAYA & MORONI. Design represents an infinite ribbon of light. Fibreglass, acrylic and car paint. Recessed LED light source provides changing colour. (H) 1670 x (W) 2005mm (66 x 79in). www.zumtobel lighteriors.com

←

Mesmeri wall-mounted light designed by Eric Solè for Artemide. Sculptural light, in painted or chromed die-cast aluminium in white or silver. (H) 154 x (W) 154 x (L) 234mm (6 x 6 x 9in). www.artemide.com

↓

Bolido suspension light by Marco Valente for Kundalini. Red, white or black silkscreened and curved glass supporting metal structure with two white glass diffusers. (H) 248 x (W) 860 x (L) 170mm (10 x 34 x 7in). www.kundalini.it

↑

Tu-Be 1 by Ingo Maurer and Ron Arad. Suspension light consisting of thirty-five aluminium tubes, which reflect light, produced by halogen and LED sources. Steel and plastic in blue and white. Dimensions for fixture: (H) 800 x (W) 500mm (31½ x 19½in). www.unicalighting.com

→

Floob floor lamp by Karim Rashid for Kundalini. Made of Plexiglas, which has translucent properties. Shown here in purple but also available in orange or transparent. Also available as table lamp. (H) 1850 x (W) 450mm (73 x 18in). www.kundalini.it

Nature floor lamp
by Diego Fortunato,
manufactured by Vibia.
Black lacquer, metal
diffuser. Also available in
red or white. (H) 1600 x
(Diameter) 500mm
(63 x 19½in).
www.vibia.es

↓
Big ceiling lamp by
Lievore, Altherr and
Molina, manufactured by
Vibia. Chrome, metacrylate
diffuser. Two sizes: 1200 x
200 and 1000 x 190mm
(47 x 8 and 39 x 7½in).
www.vibia.es

←
Samurai floor lamp
by Robby Cantarutti,
manufactured by Vibia.
Movable arm. Available in
white red or black lacquer.
(H) 2080 x (L) 2900mm
(82 x 114in).
www.vibia.es

↓

Big Bang modular wall lamp by Vicente Garcia Jiminez for Foscarini. Methacrylic sheet and aluminium organized in three different elements that can be installed individually or in combination. Various dimensions: (H) 150–950 x (L) 125–1780mm (6–37½ x 5–70in). www.foscarini.com .

→

Flower of Life chandelier by Team Two, a collaborative design from eco-architect Adam Hoets and jewellery designer Sian Eliot. Flatpack made with laser-cut stainless steel and chains. (H) 1600 x (Diameter) 500–1500mm (63 x 19½–59in). www.willowlamp.com

→

Meter by Meter by Matteo Thun. By-the-metre lighting system that can be used directly or indirectly on all interior structures from walls to ceilings. Uses energy-saving fluorescent lamps. Manufactured by the Swiss company Belux. www.belux.com

→

BiSio by Fabio Reggiani for Reggiani. Highly versatile recessed luminaire with interchangeable reflector. Fitting adjusts through 90 degrees. Built-in shade adjusts to reduce glare. (W) 235 x (D) 200–265mm (9 x 8–10½in). www.reggiani.net

←

Disk suspension light by Daniel Kubler, manufactured by Swiss company Belux. Provides energy-saving lighting. Switchable and dimmable. Aluminium and chrome. Also available as a floor lamp. (Diameter) 439mm (17in). www.belux.com

↑

Blossom by Hella Jongerius, manufactured by Belux. Each of the lights in this range has a different function: the upper opal reflector serves as general room lighting; the middle element is used for broad accentuated light; and the lowest element is a reading light. Anodized aluminium tube, stitched leather base. (H) 2115mm (83in). www.belux.com

←

Bisquit T table lamp by Ilkka Suppanen for Leucos. Double hand-blown glass diffuser. Shade available in gloss white and crystal or gloss white and wisteria. (H) 350 x (W) 350mm (14 x 14in). www.leucos.it

↑

Arca Twin Modular System by Isao Hosoe with Peter Solomon for Luxit. Range includes wall, ceiling, suspension and linear systems (as shown), providing partial downlighting. Made of metallic ABS with polypropylene covers; bearing beam is extruded aluminium. Light available in range of transparent and iridescent colours. Version shown comes in 2000mm- (79in-) long sections with two lights. (W) 220 x (L) 815mm (9 x 32in). www.luxous.com

←

RCA suspension lights by Gemma Bernal for B.Lux. Convex shade, open in both directions, polished anodized matt aluminium enclosing either fluorescent or reflective incandescent bulb. Available in two sizes. Medium: (H) 260 x (Diameter) 170mm (19 x 7in). Table, floor and wall models also available. www.grupoblux.com

→

Fold PP wall or ceiling light by R. Toso, N. Massari & Associates. Curved glass diffuser in satin white, metal front screen in polished chrome finish or in satin curved glass. Available in white, red, blue or yellow. (H) 200 x (W) 500mm (8 x 19½in). www.lightsource europe.com

←

Lantern floor lamp by Ronan and Erwan Bouroullec for Belux. Polycarbonate. Available in red, black or white combinations. (H) 1520mm (60in). www.belux.com

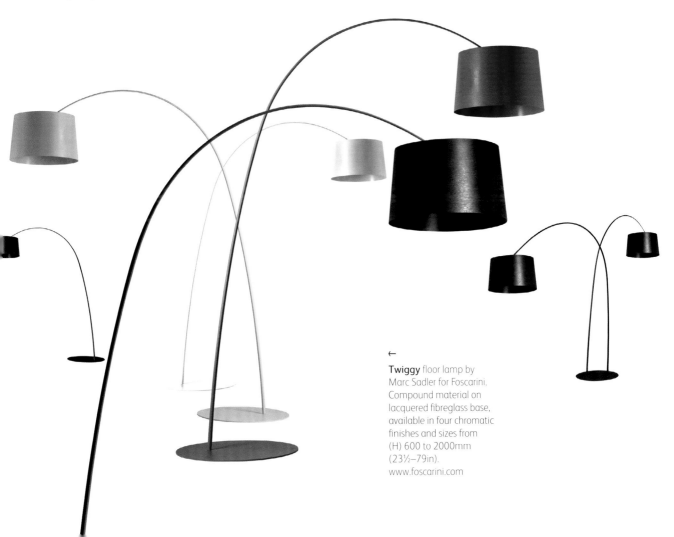

←

Twiggy floor lamp by Marc Sadler for Foscarini. Compound material on lacquered fibreglass base, available in four chromatic finishes and sizes from (H) 600 to 2000mm (23½–79in). www.foscarini.com

←

Shiny Tara polypropylene pendant light. Available in orange, grey, lilac and white. Two sizes. Small: (H) 150 x (W) 130 x (Drop) 150mm (6 x 5 x 6in). Medium: (H) 320 x (W) 280 x (Drop) 320mm (12½ x 11 x 12½in). www.ellips.de

→

Abacus Linear Silver suspension light by David D'Imperio. Anodized aluminium and stainless steel. (H) 152 x (W) 114 x (L) 1308mm (6 x 4½ x 51½in). www.daviddimperio.com

←

DNA chandelier by Benjamin Hopf and Constantin Wortmann of Buro Fur Form for Next. Polycarbonate available in any number of configurations. Other colours available. (H) 170 x (W) 135mm (7 x 5½in). www.next.de

↑

Drop ceiling suspension light by ITlab design laboratory. Manufactured by Andromeda International. Handmade Murano glass – clear Venetian crystal with blue or amber dot. Minimum height 1100 x minimum diameter 180mm (43 x 7in). www.andromedamurano.it

↑

Quadrat suspension light by Jorge Pensi. Shown here in oak laminate. Also available in natural oak or wenge. Thermo-retractable film diffuser. (L) 600 x (W) 600mm (23½ x 23½in). www.grupoblux.com

←

NE02 Nevo limited-edition table lamp by Arturo Alvarez for Arteluce. Steel frame and moulded silicone shade. Various colours. Also available as pendant and floor lamp. (H) 700 x (Diameter) 470mm (27½ x 18½in). www.arturo-alvarez.com

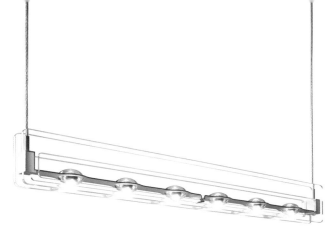

→

Gwial Aer suspension light
by Intra Lighting. Contains
six LED sources in a wood
or glass housing.
Various lengths.
www.intra-lighting.com
www.intra.si

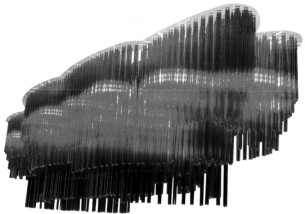

←

Big Red chandelier by
Tom Kirk. Powder-coated
steel frame, borosilicate
glass. (H) 500 x
(W) 1550mm
(19½ x 61in).
www.tomkirk.com

→

Vasi suspension light by
ITlab design laboratory.
Handmade 'incalmato'
Murano glass. Min. height
500 x min. width 150mm
(19½ x 6in).
www.itlabdesign.it

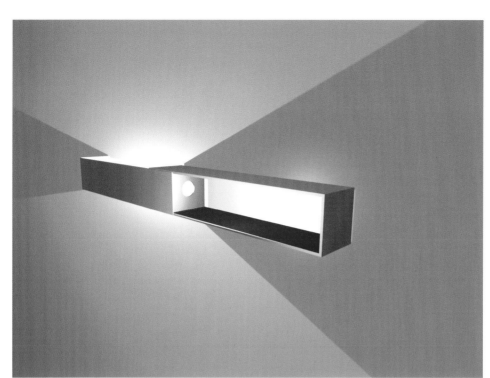

←
Donald lamp by ITlab design laboratory. Made from a folded metal slab in a square section. One element is fixed while the other mobile creates dynamic lighting effects. Variable sizes.
www.itlabdesign.it

→
Regent Channel by Felice Dittli. High-quality fluorescent system provides seamless runs of lighting, which can be concealed or surface-mounted. Light aluminium profile with integrated electrical and mechanical connectors, which can be closed with an opal or glare-free reflector. (H) 100 x (W) 90 x (L) up to 2947mm (4 x 3½ x 116in).
www.regent.ch

←
Vibia Mini Funnel ceiling light by Ramón Benedito for Vibia. Aluminium diffuser casts indirect halogen light. Available in a range of colours. (Diameter) 600mm (23½in).
www.vibialight.com

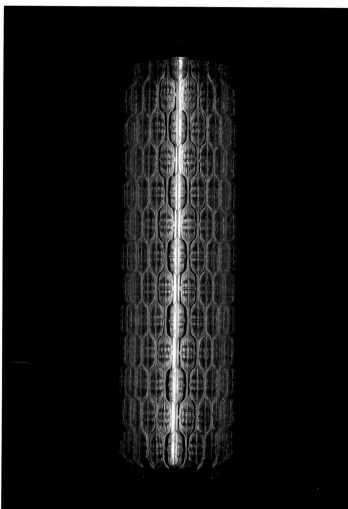

Disposable chandelier
by Stuart Haygarth. Made
from 416 disposable
plastic wine glasses with
a pink fluorescent light
source. Variety of colours
of fluorescent tubes
available. Edition of ten.
(H) 2000 x (Diameter)
500mm (79 x 19½in).
Smaller version also
available.
www.stuarthaygarth.com

Big Dish suspension light
by Ingo Maurer and team.
Fibreglass, aluminium and
steel. Blue or white.
(D) 100 x (Diameter)
480mm (4 x 19in).
www.ingomaurer.com

E.T.A. Sat suspension
light by Guglielmo
Berchicci for Kundalini.
Handmade light diffuser.
Fibreglass, polycarbonate
reflector. (H) 540 x
(D) 800mm (21 x 31½in).
www.kundalini.it

Bulb C collaboration with Swiss design group Oloom and Samuel Wilkinson, part of Bulb and Oloomette series. Available as pendant, wall or floor light. Glass with spun aluminium cap. (H) 220 x (W) 120mm (9 x 5in). www.oloom.ch.

↑
Entropia by Lionel T. Dean of FutureFactories for Kundalini. Laser-sintered nylon. (Diameter) 1200mm (47in). www.kundalini.com

→
Black Sun hanging lamp by Brian Rasmussen for Karboxx. Multi-tear shade composed of thin sheets of carbon-fibre. Also available in red or white synthetic resin. Also available in table and floor lamp versions. (Diameter) 500mm (19½in). www.brianrasmussen.org

→

Untitled pendant light
by Bruno Rainaldi.
Stainless-steel laser-cut
and enamelled white
components assembled
to interlock vertically and
horizontally. (H) 1900 x
(W) 1480 x (D) 530mm
(75 x 58 x 21in). Corner
sconce also available.
www.terzani.com

→

Re-Light adjustable
hanging light from
STENG. Fabric shade with
chrome-plated deflector,
providing two-tone
lighting in red and white.
5m (16ft) textile-covered
cable. Wall-mounted and
free-standing versions also
available. (H) 240 x
(D) 380mm (9½ x 15in).
www.steng.de

←

Luster by Ingo Maurer.
Imprinted moulded glass
containing 287 white
LEDs emitting light on
both sides, creating the
impression of three-
dimensional glass
chandelier. Available in red
and black. (H) 1000 x
(D) 650mm (39 x 25½in).
www.ingomaurer.com

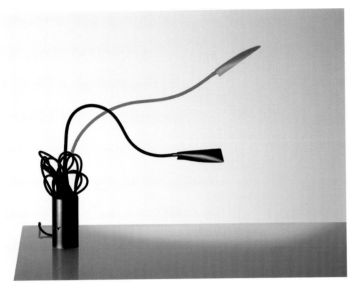

← **Kuddelmuddel** designed by Tobias Reischle for Ingo Maurer. Halogen table lamp with toggle switch and flexible arm. Metal and plastic in black and silver. Diameter of base, 80mm (3in), length of flexible arm, 700mm (27½in). Cable length 5000mm (197in). www.ingo-maurer.com

↑ **Hashi Long** designed by Naoto Fukasawa for Artemide. Table lamp fitted with miniature linear fluorescent light source. Base and arms rotate. Extruded aluminium and polycarbonate, opal white and aluminium grey. (H) 500 x (W) 185mm. www.artemide.com

→ **Light Cone** by Ingo Maurer for flush-mounting in lowered ceilings. Fibreglass available in two sizes, diameter 280 or 410mm (11 or 16in). www.ingomaurer.com

Chapter seven

HOME TECHNOLOGY

→

Jack Mama

Technology will be even more prominent in the homes of the future than it is in those of today. Indeed, home automation – a wireless control centre that turns lighting, heating and music on and off, secures doors, closes curtains, and more – is already becoming commonplace. Incorporating technology in your home is not purely a question of convenience, however; it is also about making a building more energy-efficient, and therefore it is one of the many factors that must be taken into account when constructing or renovating a house today.

Jack Mama is creative director at Philips Design, working on the Probes programme, which researches the future role of technology in people's lives – anything from five to ten to fifteen years ahead. He trained in industrial design at the Royal College of Art in London, where he was also a research fellow. 'Ever since then, I have been interested in new emerging technologies and how they are applied in the marketplace,' says Mama, who now collaborates closely with scientists and engineers. He always begins a piece of research by considering how people will be living in the future, asking himself, 'What will their values be? What will be important to them?' The next step is to 'create concepts and look at how we can facilitate those developments with technology'.

Mama says his interest in technology springs from a fascination with materials and the excitement that comes from reusing a material, an application or a manufacturing process in a different context. 'Lately, I've been preoccupied by looking at nature and biological processes,' he says, 'trying to see if we can apply some of those natural processes to technological developments.' Many people find new technology off-putting, complicated and more trouble than it's worth. No one wants to be a slave to technology and it is the job of the designer to make products user-friendly. 'When you talk to people about technology, you often end up hearing about their frustrations with it,' says Mama. 'We have a lot of work to do. Our aim is to make this stuff simpler and less challenging, so it doesn't take over our lives.'

LED (light-emitting diode) technology has transformed the potential of lighting in the home. No longer simply about illumination, lighting can now be used to alter mood or to improve health, for example – and there is an increasing number of products on the market that claim to have such effects. Mama's first project with light involved using LED technology to examine how changing colours can affect emotions. This was followed by an investigation into how certain kinds of light can be used to cleanse and rejuvenate human skin. He recently worked on the Wake Up light, a product launched by Philips in 2008, which wakes up a person gradually and more naturally than an alarm clock by using light that affects the energy hormones. He has also worked on an exploratory

concept for future light called Sunshine. 'This was a project that looked at energizing light and natural light rhythms inside the home and how the therapeutic qualities of light can enhance a sense of well-being.' Light suppresses the level of melatonin in the body. (Naturally produced by sunlight, melatonin causes drowsiness.) 'I can't say categorically that it's going to happen, but it is being explored by Philips.'

In Mama's view, the advent of broadband communications has made many of us obsessed by the issue of technology in the home. 'It's become almost invasive,' he says. 'Now that we can keep in constant touch with our loved ones and the workplace, the boundary between work and home is becoming more and more blurred. We've reached the point where the Internet is pervading many areas of our lives, as well as other communications media, such as telephones.' Different forms of technology are also invading our homes. 'The environment is on everyone's conscience these days,' says Mama. 'We're beginning to see the development of products to make us more aware of our use of energy, for example. Energy conservation on one side and how we can generate energy on the other are the things we're going to have to think about more from a technological point of view.'

Mama quotes Stephano Marzano, chief executive officer and chief creative director of Philips Design, as saying, 'The home of the future will look more like the home of the past.' Marzano has come to this view because, says Mama, 'He foresees that the black boxes in our homes will just blend into the environment and we won't even be conscious of them.' Mama laments the lack of co-ordination between technology providers and builders. 'If you're talking about the distant future – future-proofing the home – these two groups must work together. You see some elements of this, but we're still in the Stone Age as far as this stuff is concerned. Why, when you build a house, isn't there an integrated system to carry unsightly cables and utilities so they disappear into the fabric of the building? Why hasn't it been thought of in an integrated way? That's phenomenally strange to me.'

Mama believes that the most important challenge we face is sustainability. 'One of our Probe projects, Sustainable Habitat 2020, explores building methods that help to protect the environment,' he says. 'It is set in Shanghai, one of the world's most densely populated cities. The idea is to create a building with a sensitive skin, which absorbs air, light and water, and converts it into energy so it's "off the grid". Personally, I predict that products will become sensitive rather than intelligent. We are moving from labour-saving products to more dynamic, responsive environments that stimulate health and well-being. Products will disappear into the fabric of our environment and our spaces will dynamically adapt to suit us.'

←

BEL-AIR filtration system by Mathieu Lehanneur (see page 363).

→

ET20 projector with integrated DVD player by Toshiba. Extreme Short Throw (EST) projection that allows use within small spaces. (H) 155 x (W) 344 x (D) 322mm (6 x 13½ x 12½in). www.toshiba.com

← ↑

Rako RF wireless lighting controls. Digital dimming technology controls lights from anywhere in the house, saving energy. With 64,000 possible addresses and a range of up to 100m (328ft), the system can be used throughout the home. Various colours.

RDL250C and RDL500C (above) (L) 160 x (W) 50 x (D) 36mm (6 x 2 x 1½in). RPP07 (left) (L) 86 x (W) 86 x (D) 4mm (3½ x 3½ x ½in). www.rakocontrols.com

→
YSP-4000 digital sound projector by Yamaha. Connect your TV, iPod and other devices. Includes built-in FM tuner. (H) 193 x (W) 1031 x (D) 117mm (8 x 40½ x 4½in). www.yamaha.com

←
Axolute door entry system by Axolute. Can be installed anywhere in the home. Flat, liquid-crystal screen with colour LCD display, in a selection of finishes. Operates with Home Network solution to control an array of different functions. Elliptical version: (H) 185 x (W) 168mm (7 x 6½in). Rectangular version: (H) 200 x (W) 160mm (8 x 6in). www.axolute.it

↑
Studio 6 Media server by Living Control. Stores and streams music and video in a variety of formats including HD, DVD and Blu-ray or other future HD formats. Provides two independent video streams and four audio outputs for music. Can be controlled from any room. (H) 130 x (L) 300 x (D) 180mm (5 x 12 x 7in). www.livingcontrol.com

→
Touchstone control pad by Living Control. Outer ring controls volume, channel/track selection and mute; inner ring stores and recalls four settings: a favourite playlist or radio station, or any combination of light, heat, curtains, music or video. Silver or gloss black. (Diameter) 112mm (4½in). www.livingcontrol.com

←

Luxus model A retractable screen with Firehawk grey material by Stewart Filmscreens. Electronically controlled retractable screen. Variety of front- or rear-projection materials available. Tab-Guy tensioning system ensures a smooth flat-screen surface. (H) 1900 x (W) 3133mm (75 x 123in). www.stewartfilm screens.com

→

PowerLite Pro Cinema Projector 1080 UB by Epson. Features native 1080-pixel resolution for theatre-quality high-definition images. Black. (H) 120 x (W) 390 x (D) 30mm (5 x 15½ x 1in). www.epson.com

←

CineCurve curved screen by Stewart Filmscreens. Super-wide Cinemascope screen features 2.40:1 image area for optimum enjoyment when viewing movies in wide-screen formats. Horizontal masking panels glide in from the left and right to provide a perfectly masked image at any aspect ratio. (H) 1461 x (W) 3505mm (57½ x 138in). www.stewartfilm screens.com

←

Luxus Screenwall by
Stewart Filmscreens.
Fixed projection screen
with specialized front
projection. (H) 1829 x
(W) 3099mm
(72 x 118in).
www.stewartfilm
screens.com.

↓

Micropod SE speaker
system by Scandyna.
High-quality small speaker
provides big sound from
a small system. Ideal for
compact home cinemas.
Speaker available in silver,
blue, white, black, yellow or
red. (H) 195 x (W) 125 x
(D) 114mm (8 x 5 x 4½in).
Minibass also available.
www.scandyna-
speakers.com

Living Colours LED mood lamp by Philips. Can display an infinite range of colours. Choose a particular lighting effect to suit your mood. (H) 205 x (W) 170 x (D) 200mm (8 x 7 x 8in). www.philips.com

←

Incognito multi-room audio system by Cambridge Audio. Affordable high-quality system for up to four rooms. In-wall keypad: (H) x 81 x (W) 8mm (3 x ½in). Tabletop keypad: (H) 75 x (W) 119mm (3 x 4½in). Speakers: (Diameter) 142mm (5½in). www.cambridgeaudio.com

→

DMC 1000 digital media centre by Harman Kardon. Digitize, catalogue and store as many as 60,000 songs as you play them. Will also let you distribute four separate audio streams from your music library to different locations in the home. (H) 105 x (W) 440 x (D) 404mm (4 x 17½ x 16in). www.harmankardon.com

→

The amp by Scandyna. Features 2x50 watts with four stereo inputs and remote control. Floor-standing or wall-mounted. Available in silver, blue, white, black, yellow or red (H) 104mm x (Diameter) 210mm (4 x 8in). www.scandyna-speakers.com

→

BTS-01 Bluetooth speaker by Intempo. Wireless speaker system with a range of up to 10m (33ft) and 10-watt output. Automatically plays music from any compliant Bluetooth v1.2-enabled device. Silver and black. (H) 190 x (W) 280 x (D) 100mm (7½ x 11 x 4in). www.intempodigital.com

↓

Squeezebox Classic Player by Logitech. Listen to music in any room in the house. The device connects to an existing WiFi network to deliver CD-quality audio. Black. (H) 94 x (W) 193 x (D) 79mm (4 x 8 x 3in). www.logitech.com

→

SyncMaster 971P LCD monitor by Jinsun Kim and Sang-il Park for Samsung. The triple-hinge monitor allows you to choose any angle or height you wish. USB port embedded in stand for easy access. Black or white. Screen size: 480mm (19in). www.samsung.com

←

1900J TFT Fantasy Monitor by LG. Ultra-thin monitor with world's highest contrast ratio of 2000:1. Stand comes in three variations; black and red Jar model illustrated here. (H) 430 x (W) 410 x (D) 141mm (17 x 16 x 5½in). www.lge.com

→

iMac G5 by Apple. Complete, high-performance computer with ultra-thin design, includes built-in wireless capacity, Mac OS X and iLife 08. Anodized aluminium and black-bordered glass. Available in 510 and 640mm widescreen models (20 and 25in). www.apple.com

→

VPLVW60 HD home
theatre projector by Sony.
Features Sony's SXRD
panel technology and high
35,000:1 contrast ratio for
screen sizes up to 7.52m
(25ft). Anthracite. (H) 174
x (W) 395 x (D) 471mm
(7 x 15½ x 18½in.
www.sony.com

←

J10HD mini home theatre
system by LG. Plays CDs
and DVDs directly on the
integrated 80GB hard
disk. The J10HD supports
MPEG-4 and DivX videos.
High-gloss, chrome-coated
casing. Receiver unit
(H) 216 x (W) 326 x
(D) 78mm (8½ x 13 x 3in).
www.lge.com

→

MusicCast system by
Yamaha. Stores music
files for transmission
anywhere in the home.
You can also create a
playlist and access digital,
FM and Internet radio.
www.yamaha.com

DHT-FS3 X-Space Surround System by Denon. Home theatre system to connect your DVD player and TV monitor. Slim-fronted speaker unit and separate subwoofer reproduces highly ambient surround-sound. Piano black, gloss finish. (H) 96 x (W) 850 x (D) 125mm (4 x 33 x 5in). www.denon.com

←

LMD-10A51W portable DMB TV by Samsung. Up-to-date mobile TV technology closes the existing gap between a portable television and a laptop. Enjoy high-quality broadcast anywhere, entirely independent of cables or other connections. Equipped with MP3 and digital photo-viewer functions. White. 250mm (10in) LCD screen. (H) 240 x (W) 310 x (D) 30mm (9½ x 12 x 1in). www.samsung.com

→

S-302 DVD system by Denon. Hi-fi, home cinema and network in one easy-to-use system. Features full HD, Wi-Fi and Dolby Virtual Speaker, with high-quality surround-sound from just two stereo speakers. Aluminium and plastic. www.denon.com

←

FPM 6 flat panel speaker by B&W. Enclosure height matches height of 1520mm (60in) plasma screens. Can be wall- or floor-mounted. Cabinet is silver; grille comes in a variety of finishes. Wall-mounted dimensions: (H) 794 x (W) 195 x (D) 111mm (31 x 8 x 4½in). www.bowers-wilkins.co.uk

←

AirPort Express Mobile Base Station by Apple. Has super-fast 802.11n wireless technology. Lightweight, compact and easily portable. Enjoy your music library in virtually any room of the house. Shares a USB printer without obtrusive cables. (H) 95 x (W) 75 x (D) 28mm (4 x 3 x 1in). www.apple.com

↓

Connect 42 TV system by Loewe. LCD-TV with HDTV reception and DR+Direct access to all multimedia content on the home network. High-gloss white or high-gloss black. (H) 960 x (W) 680mm (38 x 27in). www.loewe-uk.com

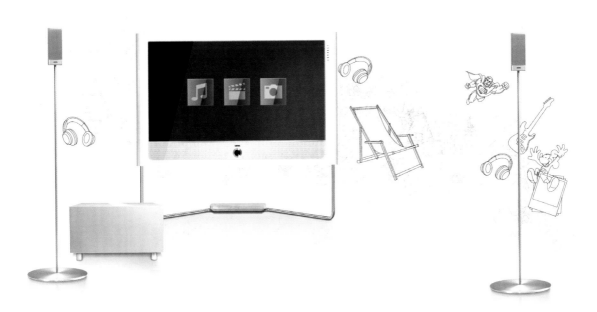

→

Eclipse TD510 speakers by Hiroshi Kowaki and Katsuhiko Taira for Eclipse TD. High-performance loudspeaker for hi-fi and home cinema. Foam ABS, zinc alloy, aluminium. Available in black, white and silver. (H) 362 x (W) 240 x (D) 345mm (14 x 9½ x 13½in). www.eclipse-td.com

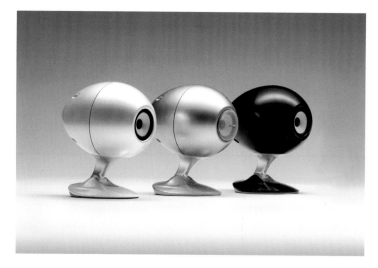

←

Clever 950 media centre by Clever Technologies. Browse the Internet, watch TV and DVDs, view stored images or listen to your music collection. Compatible with Blu-ray and HD DVD. (H) 67 x (W) 430 x (D) 340mm (2½ x 17 x 13½in). www.clevertec.co.uk

→

D10 projector by Sim2. Compact DLP video projector with short-throw lens designed to be used in smaller rooms. Available in textured matt black finish. (H) 145 x (W) 347 x (D) 316mm (6 x 13½ x 12in). www.sim2.co.uk

←

**Toshiba Regza
40RF350U** LCD
widescreen TV features
DynaLight – dynamic
backlighting for improved
contrast. High-gloss black
bezel with chrome trim.
(H) 630 x (W) 940 x
(D) 31mm (25 x 37 x 1in).
www.toshiba.com

→

C3X 1080 HD projector
from Sim2. The world's
smallest 3-chip full-HD
(1080p) DLP-based
projector. Available in four
high-gloss colour finishes.
(H) 190 x (W) 435 x
(D) 430mm
(7½ x 17 x 17in).
www.sim2.co.uk

←

LIFESTYLE V30 home-
entertainment system
by Bose. Combines
high-quality sound with
advanced technologies for
audio and video sources.
HD-compatible, works with
your existing audio and
video sources. Surround-
sound, customized to suit
room. Additional Bose
products can be connected
for listening in up to
fourteen rooms. Available
in black, silver or white.
www.bose.com

←

Boiserie Studio AV Living Wall by Listone Giordano and Massimo Iosa Ghini for Studio AV. Display for TV with storage also incorporates invisible speakers within panels. Five models in five colours, available in different shapes and sizes. www.studioav.co.uk

→

Transporter by Logitech. Wireless music system, component-style player connects to home network and plays music from your PC, iPod and the Internet. Black. (H) 77 x (W) 433 x (D) 311mm (3 x 17 x 12in). www.logitech.com

←

Katamari 01 speaker by Gyanze Design. Forged-aluminium block speaker system that houses two small drivers and an internal 15-watts-per-channel digital amplifier. The unit powers itself on when it senses an input and can also receive a Bluetooth signal. www.gyanze.com

→

Multi-room Music System
by Sonos. Wireless, digital
music system plays
music all over the house,
controlled from the palm of
your hand. White and grey.
Sonos Zoneplayer:
(H) 209.5 x (W) 260 x
(D) 113mm (8 x 10 x 4½in).
Sonos Controller:
(H) 97 x (W) 165 x
(D) 24.5mm (4 x 6½ x 1in).
www.sonos.com

→

Get Smart wireless
lighting system. Allows
you to create atmospheric
lighting in the home.
Available in black nickel,
bronze, pearl nickel,
polished chrome, polished
brass, painted white or
stainless steel. (H) 28 x
(Diameter) 92mm
(1 x 3½in).
www.getplc.com

←

Beovision 8 TV by
David Lewis for Bang &
Olufsen. Flexible solution
for TV viewing needs.
Can be used as monitor,
stand-alone TV, or in a
BeoLink set-up. White or
silver. Available in 660 or
813mm (26 or 32in).
www.bang-olufsen.com

→
New Concepts Collection
by M. Acerbis and
Massimo Castagna for
Acerbis International.
Audio-visual storage
discreetly integrates
screen, high-quality
speakers and various other
components. Comes in
three configurations and
various finishes. (H) 900
x (W) 1600 x (D) 180mm
(35½ x 63 x 7in).
www.acerbis
international.com

←
Pronto RFX9400 RF
extender by Philips.
Extends operation of your
home entertainment
system. Can be combined
with up to sixteen
extenders for wired or
wireless multi-room control
of entire home. (H) 30 x
(W) 600 x (D) 100mm
(1 x 23½ x 4in).
www.pronto.philips.com

→
Aura AV storage system
by Mab. Modular system
available in wide range of
configurations and finishes.
Wood and veneer.
www.mab-moebel.ch

←

Philips 7000 series flat panel HDTV with LED ambilight and invisible speaker technology from Philips Design Series. 500–1300mm sizes available (19½–51in). www.philips.com

←

Diabolo Sub Panel Subwoofer by Artcoustic. Complements flat-panel speakers. Can hang on the wall or stand on the floor. Slimline design in black, silver or white. (H) 500 x (W) 500 x (D) 144mm (19½ x 19½ x 6in). www.artcoustic.com

→

HTS 6515D home-theatre system by Philips. Ambisound technology features a full 5.1 multi-channel surround-sound experience through a one-piece fully integrated home theatre system that connects to a FlatTV display. iPod dock also included. Speaker: (H) 115 x (W) 336 x (D) 130mm (4½ x 13 x 5in). www.philips.com

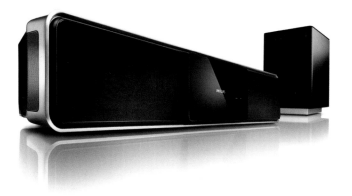

← **HTS6100 DVD** home-theatre system by Philips. Ambisound technology and full 5.1 multi-channel surround-sound experience through a one-piece, fully integrated home-theatre system that fits perfectly under a FlatTV display. (H) 153 x (W) 955 x (D) 295mm (6 x 37½ x 11½in). www.philips.com

→ **Gira SmartSensor** by Ingenhoven Architekten, Düsseldorf and Gira Designteam, Radevormwald, for Gira. Controls the functions of a room: lights can be switched, dimmed or entire scenes set, heating can be regulated and blinds raised and lowered. White, aluminium and anthracite. www.gira.com

→ **Home Automation System** by Meyer-Hayoz for Adhoco. Intelligent control unit adapts to user behaviour. Controls lights, blinds, shades, heating and ventilation in one single system. www.adhoco.com

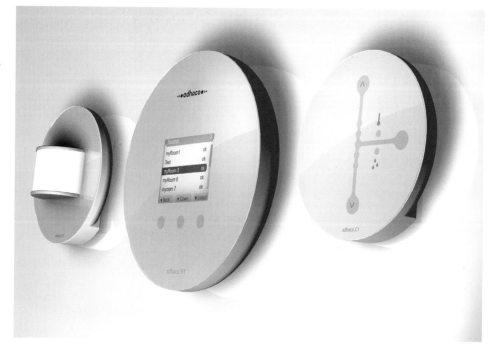

←

Entertainment and Home Cinema System Solution by Artcoustic. Plasma screen with Artcoustic 65-50 X2 left and right speakers, Artcoustic DF Multi X2 1061mm (42in) centre speaker, all mounted on Artcoustic Media Wall, which conceals cables and so on. Speaker fronts with images from Artcoustic Getty Images Gallery. Wall available in various colours and configurations. www.artcoustic.com

← ↓

TS Sensor RTR by Berker. Softouch control panel can be used to control domestic functions such as heating, air conditioning or ventilation. Integrated temperature sensor means device is also a thermostat. Glass surfaces in black, aluminium or polar white. www.berker.com

↑

Hand Transmitter HSD2 by Hörmann KG. Remote control for doors and entrance gates. Available in different finishes from aluminium-like to high-gloss chrome-plated and gold-plated. www.hoermann.com

→

E-slide drive system by Schüco International. Drive and control system with handleless design for opening, closing and locking sliding doors automatically. Aluminium. Available with remote control. Various dimensions. www.schueco.de

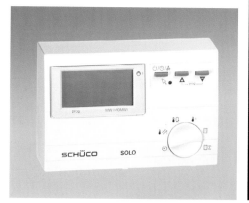

↑

DUO solar-control unit by Schüco International. Designed for use in basic and combination solar-energy systems. (H) 96 x (W) 144 x (D) 64mm (4 x 6 x 2½in). www.schueco.de

↑

Fingerprint and remote-control door system by Schüco International. Biometric fingerprint-reader system opens doors automatically. Aluminium. (H) 74 x (W) 40mm (3 x 1½in). www.schueco.de

↑

EZK electronic access control by FSB. Precision-engineered electronic key combines BlueChip technology with a range of custom-designed fittings. Aluminium, AluGray, stainless steel, bronze. Handle and key roses diameter 55mm (2in). www.fsb.de

←

Premium Line Large Module Photovoltaics
by Schüco International. Turns light into electricity. Electricity produced can be used in the building and any excess energy fed into the grid. Panels can replace standard roof materials, or be fitted on to existing roof. Frames in various colours and anodized coatings. Panel size: (H) 2152 x (W) 1252mm (85 x 49in).
www.schueco.de

HALO interactive digital video door-entry panel by Fermax. Includes clock and outside temperature thermometer. (H) 260 x (W) 140 x (D) 70mm (10 x 5½ x 3in). www.fermax.com

←
Solar storage cylinder by Schüco International. Compact design. (H) 1800 x (Diameter) 670mm (71 x 26in). www.schueco.de

→
Distribution panel pack by Digital Plumbers. Simple all-in-one wiring system for basic home automation. (H) 430 x (W) 430 x (D) 170mm (17 x 17 x 7in). www.digitalplumbers.com

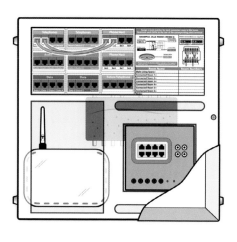

←
Solar thermal collector by Schüco International. For on-roof, in-roof and flat-roof installation, façades and canopies. Nominal heat output 2kW. Silver or bronze anodized frames, available powder-coated in a variety of colours. Two versions available. Compact line: (H) 2037 x (W) 1137 x (D) 80mm (80 x 45 x 3in). Premium line: (H) 2152 x (W) 1252 x (D) 93mm (85 x 49 x 3½in). www.schueco.de

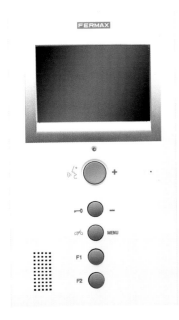

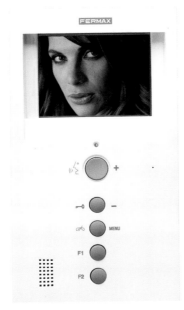

← **Loft** compact monitor by Fermax. Video door-entry panel with black and white monitor and 100mm (4in) flat screen. High-impact ABS plastic with textured finish.
www.fermax.com

← **Solar station control system** for solar energy system by Schüco International. System controls the flow of heated solar fluid to the storage cylinder or to a heating system. (H) 500 x (W) 310 x (D) 130mm (19½ x 12 x 5in).
www.schueco.de

← **Pronto PCX9200** USB music control dongle by Philips. Enables music programs on your PC to be controlled by the Pronto remote-control units.
(H) 152 x (W) 132 x (D) 38 mm
(6 x 5 x 1½in).
www.pronto.philips.com

↑ **Bathomatic** by Fredy Vasilev for Unique Automation. Digital touch-control screen bath-filler automatically fills tub to exact depth and temperature requirements pre-set by user. Can be fitted to wide variety of baths and hot-tubs. Control panel: (H) 80 x (W) 80mm (3 x 3in).
www.unique automation.co.uk

→ **Pronto TSU 9400** remote control by Philips. Wireless system controls audio-visual equipment, lighting, heating, ventilation, air conditioning and music on your PC. Provides system feedback indicating whether lights are on or off, temperature settings and weather forecast.
(H) 340 x (W) 157 x (D) 100mm
(13½ x 6 x 4in).
www.pronto.philips.com

←
Modero ViewPoint Touch Panel (MVP-5200i) by AMX. Wireless touch-screen for home automation. Combines high-resolution graphics, wireless mobility and digital intercom. (H) 120 x (W) 192 x (D) 20mm (5 x 8 x 1in). www.amx.com

→
C2N-DB Decorator Series by Crestron. Control keypad for home automation. Controls a broad range of applications from lighting to AV distribution. Variety of keypads and faceplates to suit décor. Available in black, white and almond. (H) 100 x (W) 40 x (D) 38mm (4 x 1½ x 1½in). www.crestron.com

→

BEO5 remote control by David Lewis for Bang and Olufsen. Provides touch-screen control of TV, films, music and more. System knows which devices you own and presents relevant menus and controls on its intelligent glass screen. (H) 116 x (W) 70 x (D) 33mm (4½ x 3 x 1½in). www.bang-olufsen.com

←

VIMATY 70 EIB/GLS by Vity Technologies. Wall-mounted touch-screen system for home automation centralizes all electrical controls such as KNX and pilots your infrared appliances (TV, satellites, DVD) with no external interfaces. ABS and stainless-steel frame in black and silver or white-lacquered façade. (H) 168 x (W) 234 x (D) 59mm (6½ x 9 x 2½in). www.vity.com

→

Beo Link system by Bang & Olufsen. One remote control for your entire home-entertainment system. Access to all CD, DVD and radio sources, as well as digital media, lighting and curtains. Control sound from the main room to any BeoLab loudspeakers with BeoLink Active. (H) 60 x (W) 280 x (D) 130mm (11 x 2½ x 5in). www.bang-olufsen.com

←

TSU 9600 Pronto
wireless touch-screen
for home automation
by Philips. Multi-room
control solution, works
seamlessly with its ultra-
reliable wireless extender
(RFX9400) and serial
extender (RFX9600) to
manage entertainment
equipment, content and
lighting throughout the
home. (H) 134 x (W) 206 x
(D) 203mm (5 x 8 x 8in).
www.pronto.philips.com

→

**Wall-mounted radio
transmitter** by Albrecht
Jung. Wireless home-
automation system that
requires no cables. Systems
transmitted via radio
to control lighting, air
conditioning and shading.
Ideal for retro-fitting.
Stainless steel, anthracite
and chrome. (H) 96 x
(W) 96mm (4 x 4in).
www.jung.be

→

Sentido switch by Basalte.
Touch-sensitive surface
available in two types
with two or four functions.
Illuminates at night.
Touching more than one
switch simultaneously
activates an additional
function that can switch
all lights in the room on
or off. Brushed aluminium
in chrome or black.
www.basalte.be

←

A Creation switch by Albrecht Jung. Controls brightness, blinds or temperature and radio. Surrounds and inserts available in a wide range of colours and finishes, including coloured glass and mirror finish. (H) 84 x (W) 84mm (3½ x 3½in). www.jung.be

↓

KNX room controller by Albrecht Jung. Flat design with text display controls up to twenty-four functions. Available in aluminium, stainless steel, anthracite, white, ivory and grey. (H) 167 x (W) 96mm (6½ x 4in). www.jung.be

↑

Control keypad for home automation by Hager. Room controller with four push buttons and LCD display controls and provides information about lighting, heating and so on. (H) 80 x (W) 80mm (3 x 3in). www.hager.com

→

Individual Compose 40
LCD TV by Loewe. Speaker configuration can be floor-standing. Left and right speakers attach to the TV's sides. Speaker bar runs along the TV's bottom edge. Options of compact speakers with optional floor-standing pole mounts or a full surround-sound system.
www.loewe.de

→

Automatic switch
from Jung. Switches on when movement is detected. Available in variety of finishes, with interchangeable frames. (H) 98 x (W) 98mm (4 x 4in).
www.jung.be

→

Door-entry system by Ivory Egg. With video camera or audio with wide camera angle. Available in white or gloss black. (H) 600 x (W) 220mm (23½ x 9in).
www.ivoryegg.co.uk

←

Colour touch panel
by Jung. Monitors and controls all switching operations for lights, blinds or rolling shutters, heating, air-conditioning systems, burglar alarms, signalling devices and audio components. (H) 180 x (W) 250mm (7 x 10in).
www.jung.be

← **Huministat** by Albrecht Jung. Home automation control for heating and air conditioning. Sensor monitors and adjusts moisture and temperature levels. Anthracite, aluminium or stainless steel. (H) 102 x (W) 102mm (4 x 4in). www.jung.be

↓ **Anthracite** switch by Jung. Combination of one-gang and two-gang switch. Available in wide range of finishes and colour combinations. (H) 152 x (W) 8mm (6 x ½in). www.jung.be

↑ **Owl** wireless electricity monitor by Owl. Handheld device gives up-to-the-second information on the cost of the energy you are consuming. (H) 130 x (W) 126mm (5 x 5in). www.theowl.com

←

Lutron Sivoia QS
motorized blinds
by Lutron. Can be
controlled individually
or programmed as
part of pre-set lighting
scenes. Available in
a variety of colours,
materials and sizes.
www.lutron.com

→

**Ultra-thin LCD Flat-
screen TV** from the UT
Series by Hitachi 35mm
profile. Available in 32,
37 and 42 inch 1080
HD formats.
www.hitachi.com

←

SeeTouch Keypad by
Lutron. From the 8 series,
for use with Lutron's
HomeWorks whole-home
lighting control system.
Features large easy-to-use
buttons, plus backlighting.
Customizable controls.
Available in three styles
and a wide range of
colours. (H) 117 x (W) 70 x
(D) 30mm (4½ x 3 x 1in).
www.lutron.com

←

**LG6000 LCD and plasma
TV** by LG. Features an
invisible speaker system,
specially tuned by Mark
Levinson. Incorporates
speaker actuators around
the perimeter of the bezel,
eliminating the need for
traditional speaker drivers
and associated grilles.
Black with red-coloured
back. Screen sizes: 810,
940, 1065 and 1195mm
(32, 37, 42 and 47in).
www.lge.com

→

KURO plasma PDP 508XD by Pioneer. Features include intelligent brightness control, integrated digital DVBT tuner with CI slot and multi-screen options for picture-in-picture and split-screen views. Black. 1270mm (50in) plasma screen. www.pioneer.co.uk

←

OmniTouch 5.7 Touchscreen home-control system by HAI. Adjusts lighting, heating and audio automatically. (H) 117 x (W) 150 x (D) 41mm (4½ x 6 x 1½in). www.homeauto.com

↑

Radio RA Lutron home lighting control system by Lutron. The world's first wireless radio frequency (RF) whole-home control system. Great for new or existing homes, or those under construction. No new wiring required. White or black. (H) 110 x (W) 130mm (4½ x 5in). www.lutron.com

→

SpaceStation by Blue Lounge. Docking system for laptops with internal coiling pins to conceal all cords and keep desktop tidy. Black or white. (H) 44 x (W) 108 x (L) 622mm (2 x 4 x 24½in). www.bluelounge.com

↑

Motorlight by Jake Dyson. Unique, variable-angle light – angle of beam can be increased from 8 to 60 degrees. Performs many lighting functions: uplight, floodlight, ambient and spot. White or black gloss, red, blue or clear glow. Special-edition colours on request. (H) 370 extending to 410mm (14½–16in). www.jakedyson.com

→

Majik movie system by Linn. Compact design comprising DVD player, CD player, AM/FM radio tuner, surround-sound processor, 5-channel power amplifier, Majik Movie System and Komponent 5.1 loudspeaker system. Available in silver or graphite finishes. Can also be used as part of a Linn Knekt multi-room system. Component near right: (H) 245 x (W) 180 x (D) 155mm (9½ x 7 x 6in). Component bottom centre: (H) 180 x (W) 559 x (D) 155mm (7 x 22 x 6in). www.linn.co.uk

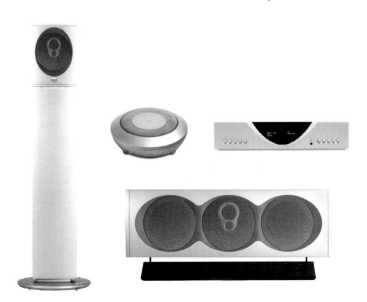

←
LCD plasma television panel by Bruno Fattorini for MDF Italia. Unit comprises open cabinets and shelving. TV can be flush-mounted or fixed to extendable arm. Matt lacquer in white or anthracite grey, natural anodized aluminium or grey oak. Available in five configurations and three lengths: 1600, 2000 or 2400mm (63, 79 or 94in). (H) 1890mm (74in). www.mdfitalia.it

↓
In-wall loudspeakers by Linn. High-performance speakers that can also be ceiling-mounted. Perfect for concealed systems. Range of performance options and sizes. White (paintable) or black. www.linn.co.uk

↓
Wireless Music Center and Station WACS7500/05 by Philips. With the stations at desired locations in your home, instantly play all your favourite music streamed wirelessly from the music centre or PC. (H) 272 x (W) 614 x (D) 172mm (10½ x 24 x 7in). www.philips.com

←
Knekt multi-room system by Linn. Lets you use and integrate up to sixteen different AV sources in one simple-to-control system. Can be accessed from any room simultaneously, via a wall-mounted or handheld remote control.
www.linn.co.uk

→
Wardrobe Care Solutions GC9920 by Philips. Integrated iron, steamer and auto-refresh mode that creates a breeze to air your garments, with innovative ironing board. Compact size: (H) 760 x (W) 500 x (D) 480mm (30 x 19½ x 19in).
www.philips.com

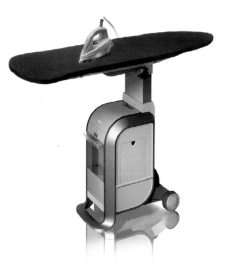

↑
Wireless music station WAK 3300 by Philips. Compact unit enables you to wirelessly access music stored on your music server or PC. Designed to be used in conjunction with Philips Music Centre. (H) 160 x (W) 175 x (D) 67mm (6½ x 7 x 2½in).
www.philips.com

amBX gaming peripherals by Philips. Surround your senses by synchronizing the in-game action with light, colour, sound, vibration and air effects to intensify the gaming experience. (H) 587 x (W) 389 x (D) 503mm (23 x 15 x 20in). www.philips.com

→

Knekt wall-mounted AV control unit by Linn. Multi-room unit features clear and simple keypad accesses and controls all music sources in your system. White or black finish. (H) 85 x (W) 146 x (D) 7mm (3½ x 6 x ½in). www.linn.co.uk

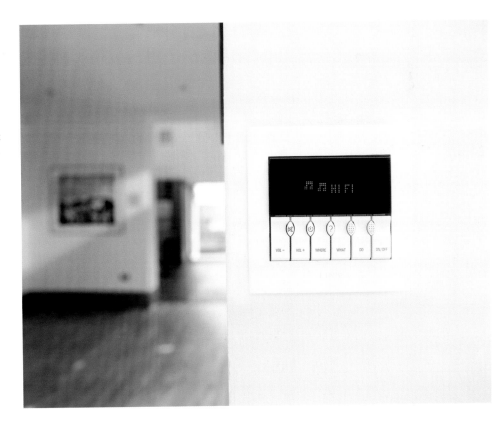

←
Sonic Chair with Audio System by Sonic Chair. Chair with two-way sound insulation that serves as an acoustic barrier between the inside and the outside. Can be connected to MP3 players and laptops. Available in 35 colours and materials such as microfibre. (H) 1440 x (W) 1200 x (D) 630mm (57 x 47 x 25in). www.sonicchair.de

→
Akurate music server by Linn. Can be accessed by up to eight users in the home, making it ideal for use in any multi-room system. Stores your entire music collection remotely on a standard networked hard drive. Can be accessed through a third-party device, such as a touchscreen or remote. (H) 44 x (W) 482 x (D) 377mm (2 x 19 x 15in). www.linn.co.uk

←
Alpha TV by Brionvega. Relaunched design classic from an orginal design by Valerio Cometti. Structure in chromed steel, plastic and tempered glass. White, orange or black. (H) 440 x (W) 517 x (D) 275mm (17 x 20 x 11in). www.brionvega.tv

→

BEL-AIR filtration system by Mathieu Lehanneur. Mini-mobile greenhouse that uses living plants to purify the air indoors. Requires no filters. White pyrex and aluminium. (H) 500 x (W) 350mm (19½ x 14in). www.mathieule hanneur.com

→

BASIK 3 IR RCU by Linn. Infrared remote control unit. Available in a choice of white, silver or black finishes. (W) 55 x (L) 94 x (D) 10mm (2 x 4 x ½in). www.linn.co.uk

←

NO1 Nulook speakers by Roland Spiegler for Nuber. Features detachable front panel with thirty-two colour options. Choose from a variety of varnish colours and real wood veneers, as well as textile cover screens in black and silver. (H) 315 x (W) 230 x (D) 165mm (12½ x 9 x 6½in). www.nubert.de

←

Muon loudspeakers by Ross Lovegrove for KEF. 6mm (½in)-thick moulded aluminium shell provides a rigid structure that minimizes any sound-distorting vibrations. (H) 2000mm (79in). www.kef.com

→

Vario entry system by Siedle. Modular system with Halogen spotlight that can be freely positioned to illuminate house number. Polished steel. Various colours. Approximately 600 x 150mm (23½ x 6in). www.siedle.de

↑

Curve 88 speakers can be customized in texture and colour to clients' individual specification. Carnival red shown here; other colours and finishes available. (H) 510 x (W) 430 x (D) 210mm (20 x 17 x 8in). www.curve88.com

→

Artcool mirror-type air conditioner by LG. Ultra-slim mirror-finish design. Features NEO Plasma. Air-purifying system pours out cool air from three sides. Various finishes including artwork. (H) 315 x (W) 1170 x (D) 173mm (12½ x 46 x 7in). www.lge.com

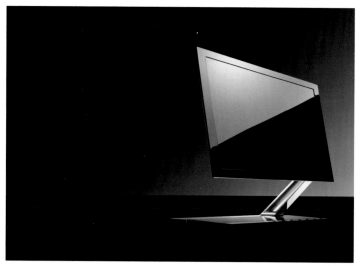

←

XEL-1 terrestrial digital/
BS/110-degree CS digital
TV by Sony. World's first
OLED (organic light-
emitting diode) TV. Gloss
black. Only 3mm at its
thinnest point. 280mm
(11in) panel. (H) 287 x
(W) 253 x (D) 140mm
(11 x 10 x 5½in).
with stand.
www.sony.net

→

The XYZ designed by
Byron Qually, Roelf Mulder
and Richard Perez for
DDDXYZ. Computer desk
with integral computer,
speakers and cable
management. Two
external ports and three
internal ports, front-
loading CDRW/DVD.
Stainless Steel and
plywood. (H) 700 x
(W) 1600 x (D) 90 mm
(27½ x 63 x 3½in).
www.dddxyz.com

←

Viteo Freewheeler
wireless outdoor speaker by Ron Arad and Francesco Pellisari for Viteo. Rechargeable, can be positioned anywhere. White, lacquered wood. (D) 250 x (Diameter) 580mm (10 x 23in). www.viteo.at

↑ →

SOLo lounge table by IF. Multifunctional furniture creates, stores and dispenses solar energy. Uses Bluetooth technology to collect, distribute and exhibit information on both the system monitor and wirelessly between computers and the Internet. Also features integrated audio amplifier with custom stereo speakers and charging points for iPods. For interior and exterior use. Stainless steel, tempered glass. (H) 460 x (W) 762 x (L) 1097mm (18 x 30 x 43in). www.intelligentforms.net

← **House-off switch** by Jack Godfrey Wood. Simple energy-saving on/off switch that allows home user to turn on and off all non-essential electronic items from a central switch. Recycled ABS. White. (H) 100 x (W) 100 x (D) 20mm (4 x 4 x 1in). www.jackgodfrey wood.co.uk

↓ **Armadi Lux** TV wardrobe by MisuraEmme. Features integrated TV and speakers housed in the thickness of the door. Glass and aluminium available in various configurations and dimensions. www.misuraemme.it

← **Monos** by Mauro Lipparini for MisuraEmme. Storage system with glass screen incorporating LCD TV that also acts as a speaker. Can be connected to any kind of hi-fi system. Glass, aluminium. Black or white. (H) 1615 x (W) 5840 x (D) 604mm (63½ x 230 x 24in). Other configurations available. www.misuraemme.it

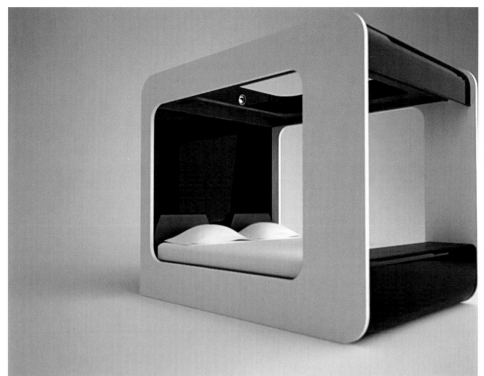

← ↓
Hi-Can High Fidelity Canopy by Edoardo Carlino for Deta. Bed that allows you to watch TV, surf the Internet, play computer games, listen to music or control all the functions of your home. Controlled by touchscreen panel in headboard or remote control. Custom-made. www.detadesign.com

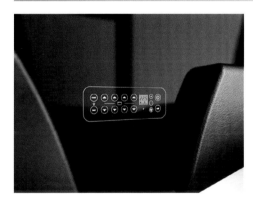

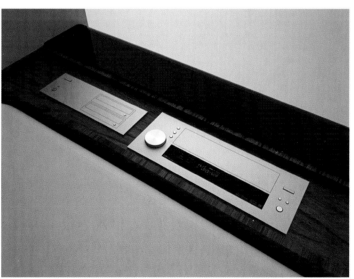

↓

VAIO VGC-LT2S by
Sony. All-in-one PC with
560mm (22in) X-black
LCD. Features 500GB,
hard drive, Blu-ray RW
and DVD-RW, motion-eye
camera, wireless keyboard
and mouse, double hybrid
TV tuner, Vista Home
Premium. (H) 418 x
(W) 643 x (D) 178mm
(16 x 25 x 7in).
www.sony.com

←

VAIO VGX TP1 by Sony.
Living room PC. Enjoy your
favourite live and recorded
TV and movies or surf the
web from your sofa – all
controlled by matching
keyboard and remote
control. Features Windows
Vista Home Premium
operating system and
300GB hard drive. Black or
white. (Diameter) 296mm
(11½in).
www.sony.com

←

Zemi Outdoor Speaker
designed by Elizabeth
Frolet & Francesco Pellisari,
part of the Viteo range,
by NACSound. Graphite,
glazed ceramic
(Diameter) 260mm (10in).
www.viteo.at

→

Doney TV by Brionvega.
Limited-edition reissue of
original design by Valerio
Cometti. Plastic and
polycarbonate in chromed
white, black or orange.
(H) 360 x (W) 330 x
(D) 36mm (14 x
13 x 1½in).
www.brionvega.tv

Index

Manufacturers' names are quoted in parentheses after the product name.

Photo credits

p.11 Federico Cedrone (Winter-Flowers-Oro-Bianco, Leopardo); p.15 Mathias Nero (Four-Leaf Clover); p.22 Christophe Fillioux (Hybride); p.36 Alberto Ferrero (Snowflake); p.40 Maarten van Houteen (Moooi carpet model01); p.41 Maarten van Houteen (Moooi carpet model 04, 05); p.48 Sebastian Szwajczak (mohohej! DIA); p.60 Paolo Veclani (Daisy White); p.62 Federico Cedrone (Corallo); p. 63 Sameli Rantanen (Flake); p.64 Helen Pe (MAJ ,ANG); p.65 Erwin Olaf (Hexagon Lace); p.69 Claudio Amadei (Flow); p.74 Claudio Amadei (Luna, Fluxos); p.100 Istvan Labady (Walchwindow04); p.100 Nabil Assaf (Option 5); p.101 Nabil Assaf (Sorrento V + Ferrara + Rondo); p.120 Anita Star (Heatwave); p.121 Schloss Möhler (Loungefire); p.126 Giorgio Di Tullio (Glossy); p.126 James Clegg (Firebelly FB); p.127 Ricciarelli (Mod.U); p.148 Franca Lucarelli/Bruno Rapisarda (Screen); p.157 Hidetoyo Sasaki (Space Heater); p.170 Maja Hollinger/Mike Meiré/Hartmut Nägele/Thomas Popinger/Heji Shin/Uwe Spoering/Thanh-Koa Tran (Kitchen Zones); p.171 Giampiero Muzzi (Nuova); p.172 Luca Fregoso (Cinqueterre); p.180 David Munoz (Compacta); p.186 Maja Hollinger/Mike Meiré/Hartmut Nägele/Thomas Popinger/Heji Shin/Uwe Spoering/Thanh-Khoa Tran (Lot); p.200 StephanAbry (Kydex); p.216 Amati Bacciardi (Mini Om); p.217 Amati Bacciardi/33Multimedia Studio (Wave,Cube,Futura); p.218 Amati Bacciardi (Platinum); p.219 Armati Bacciardi (Chrome Island, Isolabella, Concave); p.226 F2 Fotografia (Technoslide); p.229 Filippo Bamberghi/Tillmann Franzen/Jesse Frohman/Tim Giesen/Ingmar Kurth/Mike Meiré/Thomas Popinger/Heji Shin/Uwe Spoering/Thanh-Koa Tran (Sangha); p.238 Encore (Splash); p.230 Filippo Bamberghi/

Tillmann Franzen/Jesse Frohman/Tim Giesen/Ingmar Kurth/Mike Meiré/Thomas Popinger/Heji Shin/Uwe Spoering/Thanh-Koa Tran (IAM);p.238 Encore (Splash); p.240 Luca Fregoso/Maurizio Marcato/Max Zambelli (Kosmic Z2); p.243 F2 Fotografia (Technolux); p.247 Sabrina Kolb / Nico Hensel (Freeline); p.250 Ute Döring (AquaZone); p.251 Unidea di Agazzone Claudio (Touch Me); p.252 F2 Fotografia (Technostar); p.255 Federico Cedrone (Half Moon); p.257 Maurizio Marcato (Tatami); p.258 Carlo Lavatori (Geografia); p.260 Frederic Gooris/Rodrigo Torres (Alessi wall-hung WC); p. 261 Frederic Gooris/Rodrigo Torres (Alessi floor-standing washbasin); p.261 F2 Fotografia (Reverse); p.262 Maurizio Marcato (Scoop); p.264 Studio Graetz & Phaneuf Design Graphique (Saphyr); p. 267 Ottavio Tomasini; p.268 Lorenzo Barassi (XL Showerhead); p.269 Ezio Prandini (Logic Horizon); p. 274 Maurizio Marcato (Vetro); p.275 Maurizio Marcato (Light); p.291 David Sykes (Fold); p. 302 Martin Langfield (Bombay Sapphire Light); p.303 Matt Eaton (Illuminated Cornice); p.304 Amendolagine e Barracchia (PizzaKobra); p. 318 Caren Dissinger (Abacus Linear Silver suspension light); p. 318 David Steets (DNA); p.319 Cristiano Corte (Drop); p. 322 John Britton (Entropia); p.322 Tom Vack (Big Dish); p.341 Søren Jonesen (Beovision8); p.351 DA Firm (Beo Link); p. 356 Greg Rhoades (OmniTouch 5.7); p. 359 Studio Controluce (LCD Plasma TV Pamel); p.365 Brandon Bishop (Curve88); p. 366 Dean Buscher (SOLo Lounge Table); p.368 Jack Godfrey Wood (House-off switch); p.369 zone3 (Hi-Can High Fidelity Canopy).